Songs From This Earth On Turtle's Back

Contemporary American Indian Poetry

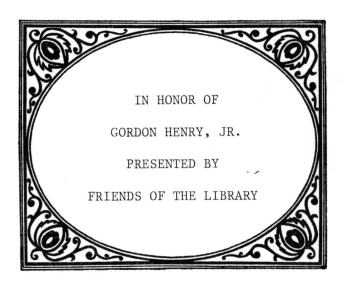

SONGS FROM
THIS EARTH
ON
TURTLE'S BACK

SONGS FROM THIS EARTH ON TURTLE'S BACK
Contemporary American Indian Poetry
Edited by Joseph Bruchac
The Greenfield Review Press

Indian Cultures
811. 54
So 58,

Publication of this book has been made possible, in part, through grants from the Literature Program of the National Endowment for the Arts and the Literature Program of the New York State Council on the Arts.

Library of Congress Cataloguing in Publication Data
Bruchac, Joseph, 1942—comp. SONGS FROM THIS EARTH ON TURTLE'S BACK
contents: Paula Gunn Allen.—Gogisgi / Carroll Arnett.—Jim Barnes. (etc.) 1. American poetry—Indian authors. 2. American poetry—20th century
Library of Congress Catalogue Card 82-82420
Greenfield Center, New York: The Greenfield Review Press

ISBN 0-912678-58-5

FIRST EDITION

Cover illustration by Kahionhes (John Fadden)

6-20-90   *Gift*   *10.95*

ACKNOWLEDGEMENTS

Some of the poems in this book have previously appeared in the following publications. In all cases, permission to reprint has been granted to the publisher by the individual authors. The importance of these magazines and publishers cited on the following pages cannot be stressed strongly enough. We gratefully acknowledge their role in the development and continuance of contemporary Native American writing.

Cover Drawing by John Kahionhes Fadden.

Paula Gunn Allen: *Coyote's Daylight Trip,* La Confluencia, 1978 for "Grandmother." *Shadow Country,* UCLA Native American Series, 1982 for "Recuerdo," "Powwow 79, Durango." *A* for "Kopis'taya." *Frontiers,* Vol. Vi., No. 3 for "Pocahontas to her English Husband, John Rolfe."

Carroll Arnett/Gogisgi: *Rounds,* Cross Cultural Communications, 1982 for "Ayohu Kanogisdi," "Bio-Poetic Statement," "Song of the Breed." *South Line,* The Elizabeth Press, 1979 for "The Old Man Said."

Jim Barnes: *The American Book of the Dead,* University of Illinois, 1982 for "Autobiography, Chapter XVII: Floating the Big Piney," and "Concomly's Skull." *The Fish On Poteau Mountain,* Cedar Creek Press, 1980 for "Four Choctaw Songs," and "Wolk Hunting Near Nashoba."

Peter Blue Cloud: *Turtle, Bear & Wolf,* Akwesasne Notes, 1976 for "To-ta Ti-om." *White Corn Sister,* Strawberry Press, 1979 for "Dogwood Blossoms." *Elderberry Flute Song,* The Crossing Press, 1982 for "Sweat Song," "Coyote, Coyote, Please Tell Me," and "Elderberry Flute Song."

Beth Brant: *The Greenfield Review,* Volume 10, Number 1 & 2 for "for all my Grandmothers." *Corridors,* Volume 3, Number 1. Spring 1982 for "Ride The Turtle's Back." *Sinister Wisdom* #17, Summer 1981 for "Native Origin."

Diane Burns: *Riding The One-Eyed Ford,* Strawberry Press, 1981 for "Gadoshkibos," "Big Fun."

Barney Bush: *Petrogylphs,* Greenfield Review Press, 1982 for "Another Old Song."

Gladys Cardiff: *To Frighten A Storm,* Copper Canyon Press, 1976 for "Long Person," "To Frighten a Storm," "Tlanusi'yi, The Leech Place," "Combing," "Owl And Rooster."

Robert J. Conley: *21 Poems,* Aux Arcs Press, 1975 for "*Wili Woyi.*" *Quetzal* for "Ned Christie." *The Beloit Poetry Journal* for "The Hills of *Tsa-la-gi.*" *The Remembered Earth,* University of New Mexico, 1981 for "The Rattlesnake Band."

Charlotte DeClue: *Without Warning,* Strawberry Press, 1983 for "Morning Song," "Yesterday Robin spoke to me . . . ," "Place-of-Many-Swans," "Ijajee's Story." *That's What She Said,* anthology of Indian women's writing, edited by Rayna Green. *Sinister Wisdom,* issue on Indian women, edited by Beth Brant.

Anita Endrezze-Danielson: *Burning The Fields,* Confluence Press, 1983 and *The North People,* Blue Cloud Quarterly, 1983.

Nia Francisco: *Suntracks,* Volume 6 (*The South Corner of Time*), 1980 for "Morning and Myself." *The Remembered Earth,* edited by Geary Hobson, University of New Mexico, 1981 for "men tell and talk."

Diane Glancy: *Calyx, A Journal of Art and Literature by Women* for "Lunar Eclipse."

Janet Campbell Hale: *Custer Lives in Humboldt County,* The Greenfield Review Press, 1978 for "Backyard Swing," "Custer Lives in Humboldt County," "Desmet, Idaho, March 1969."

Joy Harjo: *What Moon Drove Me To This,* I. Reed Books, 1979 for "Crossing The Border Into Canada." *She Had Some Horses,* Thunder's Mouth Press, 1983 for "Anchorage," "Remember," "New Orleans," "She Had Some Horses."

Lance Henson: *Buffalo Marrow On Black,* Full Count Press, 1980 for "buffalo marrow on black," "north," and "at chadwicks bar and grill."

Geary Hobson: *Southwest: A Contemporary Anthology* for "Going To The Water." Strawberry Press Broadside in *From The Center*: "Tiger People."

Linda Hogan: *Calling Myself Home,* Greenfield Review Press, 1978 for "Song For My Name," "Blessing." *Daughters, I Love You,* Loretto Heights, 1980 for "Black Hills Survival Gathering, 1980," Massachussetts Review for "Saint Coyote."

Karoniaktatie / Alex Jacobs: *Akwesasne Notes,* Vol. 6, No. 3, July 1974 for "Elegy."

Maurice Kenny: *Dancing Back Strong The Nation,* White Pine Press, 1978 for "Going Home," "Wild Strawberry. *The Smell of Slaughter,* The Blue Cloud Quarterly, 1982 for "They Tell Me I Am Lost," "Cornplanter."

Tauhindauli / Frank LaPena: Strawberry Press Broadside in *From The Center,* 1983: "Waiting For A Second Time."

Harold Littlebird: *On Mountain's Breath,* Tooth of Time Books, 1982 for "If You Can Hear My Hooves," "After The Pow-wow," "Coming Home in March," "Hunter's Morning," and "A Circle Begins."

Adrian C. Louis: *The Greenfield Review,* Volume 9, Nos 3 & 4 for "The Walker River Night."

Phillip Yellowhawk Minthorn: *Vigil of the Wounded,* Strawberry Press, 1983. *Spawning The Medicine River* for "From Which War," and "Vigil of the Wounded."

N. Scott Momaday: *The Gourd Dancer,* Harper and Row, 1976 for "The Delight Song of Tsoai-Talee," "The Gourd Dancer," "The Colors of Night," The Eagle Feather Fan," "The Fear of Bo-talee."

Duane Niatum: *Digging Out The Roots,* Harper and Row, 1977 for "Digging Out The Roots," "Street Kid," "Songs From The Maker of Totems." *Ascending Red Cedar Moon,* Harper and Row, 1973 for "Chief Leschi of the Nisqually."

Nila Northsun: *Small Bones/Little Eyes,* Duckdown Press, 1981 for "up & out." *Native Nevadan* for 'the sweat," "the red road."

William Oandasan: *A* for "Round Valley Reflections," "The Past," and "The Song of Ancient Ways."

Louis (LittleCoon) Oliver: *Caught in a Willow Net,* The Greenfield Review Press, 1983 for all selections included.

Simon J. Ortiz: *Going For The Rain,* Harper and Row, 1976 for "My Father's Song." *Fight Back: For the Sake of the People, For the Sake of the Land,* INAD, 1980 for "A New Story." *From Sand Creek,* Thunder's Mouth Press, 1981 for the selection from that book.

Rokwaho: *Contact II* for "Owl." Akwesasne Notes Calendar, 1982 for "amber the sky . . ."

Wendy Rose: *Lost Copper,* Malki Museum Press, 1980 for "The well-intentioned question," and "How I came to be a graduate student." *Contact II* for "Sarah; Cherokee Doctor." *Ms Magazine* for "Julia."

Norman H. Russell: *Come To Power,* Dick Lourie, Ed., The Crossing Press, 1974 for "The Tree Sleeps In Winter."

Ralph Salisbury: *Going To The Water,* Pacific House Publishers, 1982.

Leslie Silko: *Laguna Woman,* The Greenfield Review Press, 1974 for "Toe'osh: A Laguna Coyote Story," and "Where Mountainlion Laid Down With Deer." *Storyteller,* Seaver Books, 1981 for "Story From Bear Country."

R. T. Smith: *Dancy* for "The Long Joke," *Sanskrit* for "Yonosa House."

Mary TallMountain: *There Is No Word For Goodbye,* Blue Cloud Quarterly, 1981 for "Indian Blood," "There is no Word for Goodbye," and "Good Grease."

Luci Tapahonso: *One More Shiprock Night,* Tejas Art Press, 1981 for "The Belly of the Land," and "The Dust Will Settle." *Seasonal Woman,* Tooth of Time Books, 1982 for "Hills Brothers Coffee."

Earle Thompson: *The Prison Writing Review,* Winter 1982/83 for "Song," "Mythology," and "Winter Count . . ." *Oklahoma Camp Crier* for "Woman Made of Stars," *Northwest ARts* for "The Corral."

Laura Tohe: *Reciembra,* 1982 for "The Shooting," and "To Shimá sani."

James Welch: *Riding The Earthboy 40,* Harper and Row, 1976 for all selections included.

Roberta Hill Whiteman: *Star Quilt,* Holy Cow Press, 1983 for all selections included.

Elizabeth Woody: *Spawning The Medicine River,* 1982 for "Eagles," "Night Crackles," and "Custer Must Have Learned To Dance."

Ray A. Young Bear: *Winter of the Salamander,* Harper and Row, 1980 for all selections included.

The following Publishers and Magazines deserve special attention for their continuing service to contemporary American Indian publishing. They deserve your attention and support:

A: A Journal of Contemporary Literature, edited by William Oandasan, Box 42A510, York Station, California 90042.

Akwesasne Notes, Sotsisowah, Editor, Mohawk Nation, Rooseveltown, N.Y. 13683.

The Blue Cloud Quartery, edited by Brother Benet Tvedten, Blue Cloud Abbey, Marvin, South Dakota 57251.

Contact/II, edited by Maurice Kenny and J. G. Gosciak, P.O. Box 451, Bowling Green Station, NYC 10004.

Spawning The Medicine River, Phil Foss, Editor, Institute of American Indian Arts. St Michaels Drive, Santa Fe, N.M. 87501.

Sun Tracks: An American Indian Literary Series, Larry Evers, Editor, English Department, University of Arizona, Tucson, Az. 85721.

Harper and Row's Native American Publishing Program, Harper and Row Publishers, 10 East 53rd Street, NYC 10022.

Native American Series, William Oandasan, Editor, American Indian Studies Center, University of California, Los Angeles, Los Angeles, Ca.

Strawberry Press, Maurice Kenny, Editor, P.O. Box 451, Bowling Green Station, NYC 10004.

For Our Children

CONTENTS

SONGS FROM
THIS EARTH ON TURTLE'S BACK: An Introduction

Once, the story goes, a woman fell from the land in the sky. She fell through a hole made by the uprooting of a great tree and as she fell she grasped in her palm a handful of seeds. Down she fell, a long long way. Below her there was no Earth, only the ancient waters and in those waters birds and animals swam.

"Look," they said, "Someone is coming." Then some of the birds—Swans or Geese—flew up to catch her on their wings. Below the other creatures held council. "There must be a place for her to stand," they said. "We must bring up Earth." So, one after another, they dove down to try to bring up some mud from below that ancient sea. All of them failed but the last one—Muskrat. It brought up a tiny pawful of wet dirt.

"Now where shall we place it?" they said.

"Place it on my back," a deep voice answered. It was the Great Turtle swimming up from the depths. When they placed the earth on Great Turtle's back it grew larger and larger until it became this continent on which we stand, this Earth on Great Turtle's back. There Sky Woman was placed by the birds. There she dropped the seeds which grew into the good plants. So that story of Creation begins.

It is a very old story, but to some it is as new and real as if it happened yesterday. It reminds them of the interconnected nature of all things, that we humans—grandchildren of Sky Woman—exist because of and in relationship to all of the living world around us. The earth beneath our feet is alive. (And modern geological theory—with ideas of plate tectonics and continental drift—conforms well to that imagery of a living land on the back of a great slow animal.) It is more than a beautiful myth, it is a legend to live by.

The story of Sky Woman is an American Indian story and this anthology of poems by writers from more than 35 different Native American nations has grown from the soil of Turtle Island like the seeds fallen from Sky Woman's hand. It is a collection of contemporary writers, not a compilation of chants or songs put together in the 19th century by a non-Indian ethnologist or "retranslated" by a contemporary non-Indian writer. There are already many anthologies of those two last types. They reinforce the beliefs, held by all too many people in both Europe and the United States, that American Indian literature consists solely of traditional oral poetry and that this oral poetry and the people who created it belong to the past. The heritage of American Indian oral literature (which is still very much alive today—from the Gai'wi-io of the Iroquois to the Nightway Chant of the Navajo) is a truly great one. If anything, its real range, meaning and contemporary relevance have not yet been explored. (One of the better contemporary books which offers an approach to these oral traditions is Karl Kroeber's TRADITIONAL AMERICAN INDIAN LITERATURES, University of Nebraska Press, 1981.) Frequently the texts are available only in inaccurate translation or new "versions" which present the work out of context. The work now being done by Native American people themselves on their oral traditions should, in the next few years, bear some very interesting fruit. Ray Young Bear is engaged in an oral literature project, collecting stories from native people in the midwest. However, that large body of oral traditions should not be allowed to eclipse the achievement of the new generations of Native American writers. In the last two decades these men and women have created remarkable works of poetry and prose. Like the poems in this collection, nearly all of that new work has been written in English. N. Scott Momaday, a Kiowa writer who won the Pulitzer Prize in 1969 for his novel, HOUSE MADE OF DAWN, is one of those writers, but he is only one of many and not the first Native American to achieve success as a writer. The history of written literature in English among the Cherokee alone goes back more than 150 years. The Sioux writer Charles Eastman won international reknown for his autobiographical writings, including FROM THE DEEP WOODS TO CIVILIZATION and INDIAN BOYHOOD, at the turn of the century. And there are many others.

Today there are hundreds of Native American people whose poems, plays and creative prose have appeared in magazines, anthologies and individual collections. Their work is greatly varied and that variety should be evident in this anthology—from the lyric and mysterious voice of the Cheyenne writer Lance Henson (who acknowledges his debt as a poet to both non-Indian—such as the Spanish poets Lorca and Jiminez—and Indian traditions) to the sometimes bitter realism of Hopi/Miwok Wendy Rose. Their sources range from old stories to contemporary political and social issues familiar to any citizen of the "global village." However, varied as they may be (and rightly so, since they come from many parts of a vast continent and from nations often as different one from the other as the Welsh are from the Basque—to name only two modern non-Indian "tribes") they share certain things, things shared by all American Indian people.

They share traditions of respect for the Earth and the natural world; viewing themselves as part of, not apart from or in dominion over, the natural creation. They share strong folk cultures which have either been transmitted to them by family or learned through a continuing personal seeking. They share respect for the awesome power of the Word—power which can make or destroy, break or heal. Some of them share the experience of growing up with a first language other than English and all of them are aware that English—no matter how much they have mastered it and made it their own—will always be a different language for them than it is for the average American writer. For these poets English is a language brought by those who dispossessed them. It is also now a language of American Indian people, a carrier of their own and their people's dreams and visions. They all share the experience of being viewed as outsiders in their own land, stereotyped and misunderstood, more invisible than Ellison's INVISIBLE MAN. They also share a high level of accomplishment, for they are among the best American poets and—to my mind at least—among the best writers of today in the English language. Many of them will be found represented in two other contemporary anthologies which I recommend: Duane Niatum's 1975 anthology of Native American poetry, CARRIERS OF THE DREAM WHEEL (Harper and Row) and Geary Hobson's important general anthology of American Indian writing THE REMEMBERED EARTH (University of New Mexico Press, 2nd printing, 1980).

For a time, it seemed as if the Native Americans were a dying people. If anything, that was the aim of certain administrations in the past (and, perhaps, today) in the United States. Current demographic studies indicate that the Native American population of North America alone was far greater before the arrival of Europeans than was originally thought. There may have been as many as 50 million American Indian people here in the 1400's. Thus, the extent of the genocide which ensued was truly incredible. Population figures for American Indian people in the United States in the early 1900's indicated there were less than half a million left! However, the decline of American Indian people has ended. The 1960 census showed 750,000. The 1980 census showed 1,500,000. And that vitality—as well as a deep awareness of the bitter past—shows in the poems you are about to read.

It is my hope that this book will serve as an introduction and will lead to further reading. American Indian writers have a great deal to offer, not just to their own people, but to all human beings who believe in the Earth, in the survival of living things, in the survival of the spirit. Let us listen carefully to their words, these songs from this Earth on Turtle's back.

Joseph Bruchac
Maple Sugar Moon, 1983

Paula Gunn Allen

A couple of years ago I got a new friend, and over the next few months we talked a lot. I told her all sorts of things about my life, about how I was raised. Made jokes and observations, commenting on the life around me. At last she said, "No wonder your writing is obscure! Your life is obscure!" She meant, of course, obscure if read from a mainstreet USA point of view. And of course, she's right, that poet girlfriend of mine.

When you're a halfbreed, a daughter of both Laguna and Lebanon; when you're raised in Cubero where almost everyone speaks Spanish, New Mexico style; when your grandaddy is Jewish from Germany—not Orthodox, not Reformed, just born of Jews; when your whole family's lives are obscure in America, revised, disappeared; when you think Main Street is a small dusty road that winds its way Uptown—to the rest of the small village you call home; when only one of the five languages your family converses in is English—you're bound to be a bit challenging to understand. And when your mother is a daughter of the last gynocracy on earth, and your father a son of an ancient patriarchy, you're bound to write difficult poetry; you're bound to be a bit of an oddity in America, or anywhere at all.

My poetry, my poetics and my aesthetics all arise out of this chaotic mix, this primordial soup. Melting pots hold no terrors for me because I am one. But the thing about soup, well prepared, is that no flavor is blurred or destroyed. Rather, each flavor is heightened and enhanced, particularized, by the presence of all the rest. I think poetry is a soup. I think poetry is food. I think a poetics that operates like life engendering cooking operates, with knowledge of good ingredients, concentration, training and real knowledge of food, of mixtures that work and mixtures that don't—and above all, of food as nourishment, would be a fine and

1

useful poetics. And I think a useful poetics would be a good thing to have in this 1983-on-the-way-to-whereever world I live in now.

When I read a poem I look for several things: I want right away to know what it says. The purely decorative is of little interest to me. I want also to know what it feels. I want to know how *it is. (As distinguished from* What *it is.) I want to know who its mother is; that is, what context it comes out of. Only a few pieces of literature come out of Cubero or Laguna/Acoma, for instance, and I seldom make the error of thinking they should live up to our local standards if they are to be good poems. I never make the error of designating what is true in Cubero as "Universal," though I suppose I should because hardly anything of worth goes on anywhere that does not go on there. McLeish opined that "a poem should not mean but be," and Jan Clausen said that poetics of use is not possible and is a dangerous notion.[1] But where I come from beautiful and useful are synonomous, and useful is always* beauty full, *always meaningful, given the context, given that one knows who is the mother of the item under consideration. I think a world that does not want meaning or use is a very strange world for a human being to operate in, though having seen New York City I can understand how one can come to such a pass. I cannot imagine a meal that is not of use, and thus beautiful; I cannot imagine a meal that is without meaning. I cannot imagine wanting such a meal which is no meal at all but a cruel fraud, like having a mother who never was, and who never meant to be, one who died before you were conceived.*

I am not arguing here for a "utilitarian" poetics, because utilitarianism is a European-industrial notion that has no meaning in Cubero where there are no factories, only mountains, plains, mesas, and creatures large and small, human and otherwise. But I am arguing that language has potential. Power. I think, like my Laguna people do, that transformation is not only possible through proper use of language, but is inherent to it. Language, like a woman, can bring into being what was not in being; it can, like food, transform one set of material into another set of material. I think poetry, properly done, is both mother and food, like being the halfbreed Laguna/Lebanese I am is mother and nourishment of what I write and of what I do.

---

[1] *Jan Clausen,* A Movement of Poets: Thoughts on Poetry and Feminism *Brooklyn, Lang Haul Press, 1982, p. 22-23. She is discussing remarks of Judy Grahn and Karen Brodine (two writers whose understandings about poetics and politics are very different, by the way).*

Grandmother

Out of her own body she pushed
silver thread, light, air
and carried it carefully on the dark, flying
where nothing moved.

Out of her body she extruded
shining wire, life, and wove the light
on the void.

From beyond time,
beyond oak trees and bright clear water flow,
she was given the work of weaving the strands
of her body, her pain, her vision
into creation, and the gift of having created,
to disappear.

After her,
the women and the men weave blankets into tales of life,
memories of light and ladders,
infinity-eyes, and rain.
After her I sit on my laddered rain-bearing rug
and mend the tear with string.

Pocahontas to her English husband, John Rolfe

Had I not cradled you in my arms,
oh beloved perfidious one,
you would have died.
And how many times did I pluck you
from certain death in the wilderness—
my world through which you stumbled
as though blind?
Had I not set you tasks
your masters far across the sea
would have abandoned you—
did abandon you, as many times they
left you to reap the harvest of their lies;
still you survived oh my fair husband
and brought them gold
wrung from a harvest I taught you
to plant: Tobacco. It
is not without irony that by this crop
your descendents die, for other powers
than those you know take part in this.
And indeed I did rescue you
not once but a thousand thousand times
and in my arms you slept, a foolish child,
and beside me you played,
chattering nonsense about a God
you had not wit to name;
and wondered you at my silence—
simple foolish wanton maid you saw,
dusky daughter of heathen sires
who knew not the ways of grace—
no doubt, no doubt.
I spoke little, you said.
And you listened less.
But played with your gaudy dreams
and sent ponderous missives to the throne
striving thereby to curry favor
with your king. I saw you well. I
understood the ploy and still protected you,
going so far as to die in your keeping —
a wasting, putrifying death, and you,
deceiver, my husband, father of my son,
survived, your spirit bearing crop
slowly from my teaching, taking
certain life from the wasting of my bones.

Kopis'taya
(a Gathering of Spirits)

Because we live in the browning season
the heavy air blocking our breath,
and in this time when living
is only survival, we doubt the voices
that come shadowed on the air,
that weave within our brains
certain thoughts, a motion that is soft,
imperceptible , a twilight rain,
    soft feather's fall, a small body
dropping into its nest, rustling, murmuring,
settling in for the night.

Because we live in the hardedged season,
where plastic brittle and gleaming shines
and in this space that is cornered and angled,
we do not notice wet, moist, the significant
drops falling in perfect spheres
that are the certain measures of our minds;
almost invisible, those tears,
soft as dew, fragile, that cling to leaves,
petals, roots, gentle and sure,
every morning.

We are the women of daylight; of clocks and steel
foundries, of drugstores and streetlights,
of superhighways that slice our days in two,
Wrapped around in glass and steel we ride
our lives; behind dark glasses we hide our eyes,
our thoughts, shaded, seem obscure, smoke
fills our minds, whisky husks our songs,
polyester cuts our bodies from our breath,
our feet from the welcoming stones of earth,
Our dreams are pale memories of themselves,
and nagging doubt is the false measure of our days.

Even so, the spirit voices are singing,
their thoughts are dancing in the dirty air.
Their feet touch the cement, the asphalt
delighting, still they weave dreams upon our
shadowed skulls, if we could listen.
If we could hear.
Let's go then. Let's find them. Let's
listen for the water, the careful gleaming drops
that glisten on the leaves, the flowers. Let's
ride the midnight, the early dawn. Feel the wind
striding through our hair. Let's dance
the dance of feathers, the dance of birds.

Powwow 79, Durango

haven't been to one in almost three years
there's six drums and 200 dancers a few
booths piled with jewelry and powwow stuff
some pottery and oven bread
everyone gathers
stands for the grand entry
two flag songs
and the opening prayer by some guy
works for the BIA
who asks our father
to bless our cars
to heal our hearts
to let the music here tonight
make us better, cool
hurts and unease
in his son's name, amen.
my daughter arrives, stoned,
brown face ashy from the weed,
there's no toilet paper
in the ladies room she accuses me
there's never any toilet paper
in the *ladies* room at a powwow she glares
changes
calms
its like being home after a long time
are you gonna dance I ask
here's my shawl
not dressed right she says
the new beaded ties I bought her swing
from her long dark braids
why not you have dark blue on I say
look.
we step inside the gym
eyes sweep the rubber floor
jackets, jeans, down-filled vests,
sweatshirts all dark blue.
have to look close to pick out
occasional brown or red on older folks
the dark brown faces rising on the bleachers
the dark hair on almost every head
ever see so many Indians
you're dressed right
we look at the bleachers
quiet like shadows
the people sit watching the floor below
where dancers circle the beating drums
exploding color in the light.

Recuerdo

I have climbed into silence trying for clear air
and seen the peaks rising above me like the gods.
That is where they live, the old people say.
I used to hear them speak when I was a child
and we went to the mountain on a picnic
or to get wood. Shivering in the cold air then
I listened and I heard.

Lately I write, trying to combine sound and memory,
searching for that significance once heard and nearly lost.
It was within the tall pines, speaking.
There was one voice under the wind—something in it
that brought me to terror and to tears. I wanted
to cling to my mother so she could comfort me,
explain the sound and my fear, but I simply sat,
frozen, trying to feel as warm as the campfire,
the family voices around me suggested I should.

Now I climb the mesas in my dreams.
The mountain gods are still, and still I seek.
I finger peyote buttons and count the stalks of sweetsage
given me by a friend—obsessed with a memory
that will not die.
I stir wild honey into my carefully prepared cedar tea
and wait for meaning to arise,
to greet and comfort me.

Maybe this time I will not run away.
Maybe I will ask instead what that sounding means.
Maybe I will find that exact hollow
where terror and comfort meet.
Tomorrow I will go back and climb the endless mesas
of my home. I will seek thistles drying in the wind,
pocket bright bits of obsidian and fragments
old potters left behind.

Photo by Michael Johnston

Gogisgi / Carroll Arnett

Carroll Arnett/Gogisgi was born in Oklahoma City in 1927 of Cherokee-French ancestry. His poems and stories appear in many publications and have been collected in nine books, most recent of which are ROUNDS (Cross Cultural Review Chapbook, 1982), SOUTH LINE (1979), and TSALAGI (1976), the last two published by the Elizabeth Press. Winner of an NEA Fellowship in Creative Writing, he has edited a special American Indian issue of The Beloit Poetry Journal *and is a co-editor of the new series of Coyote's Journal, the first number of which was published by Wingbow Press in 1982. Educated (as he puts it) "by twenty-one months in the Marine Corps and later at the University of Oklahoma, Beloit College, and the Unviersity of Texas," he teaches literature and writing at Central Michigan University and lives with his wife, Claudia, on a fifty-acre farm near Mecosta, Michigan.*

Bio-Poetic Statement:
Instruction to Warriors on Security

Do not take your piece
off safety until,
as They Say, Clear and
Present Danger to Your
Life or Other Innocent
Lives is imminent.

If you must
hit him,
aim low.

If you hit him
in the head or
in the chest,
you will likely kill him,
and we do not want
to do that.

If you hit him
in the belly or
in the legs,
you will likely stop him,
and we do want
to do that.

If you hit him
anywhere else or
miss,
you have wasted
ammunition, and
we have none to waste.

*I write
in exactly
this way.*

Ayohu Kanogisdi
Death Song

aya ahaniquo
I am here only

usdi nahiyu
a little while

ayagvgeyu
I have loved

ulihelisdi elohi
the joy of the earth

osiyo ayohu
hello death

The Old Man Said

Some will tell
you it doesn't
matter. That is
a lie. Everything,
every single thing
matters. And
nothing good
happens fast.

The old man said

The wisdom of an
animal may be
measured by
the quantity of its
excrement.
              See
how little of his
waste brother deer
leaves behind.

The old man said

Indian people were not
made to live in
cities, and none do.
Some reside there
but none live there.

The old man said

"For bringing us
the horse we could
almost forgive you
for bringing us
whiskey."
    Almost.

   wado Lame Deer

The old man said

When a woman
offers you the pleasure
of coming with her,
you must be able
to tell her and
yourself, I respect
this gift as much
as I want it
or I would not
accept it. If
you cannot say
this, it is mere
disposal and shameful.

The old man said
when asked

*And when was your
grandson born?*

He was born in
nineteen and
forty-one.

*What day of
what month?*

Well I sure don't
know what day
it was, but I do
re-collect it
was in the late spring
of the year when
the sweet corn was just
four inches high.
He was born on
that day.

And?

They took him in
the army and sent him
overseas and then
he got himself
killed.

The old man said

It is never done with
the old people nor
the young nor those
sick in their bodies,
sick in their heads.

It is never done with
strangers who accept
food or rest and
offer back good will.

It is never done with
an enemy who submits.

It is done only with
those who betray the people,
those flagrant in trading
themselves or their bodies,
those taking profit upon
their grandfathers, grandmothers,
brothers or sisters,
any father mother brother sister
who walks crawls flies swims
sits or stands.

It is done only with
those who waste.

They are not wasted,
they are thrown away.

Look Back

I listen to this
86 year old
whiteman chuckle about
years ago when he
and the other boys
dug up Seminole
graves and used the skulls
for target practice.

I listen, say
nothing, leave the room
quietly. I am
supposed to respect
this man who is
my wife's father.

I listen, knowing
this old man who
is so kind to
his family, who
fears so much but
respects nothing,
will soon be gone.

Still listening,
knowing something
is going to happen,
something bad
is going to happen,
something bad
is going to keep on
happening.

Last May

I watched two
barn swallows swoop
the field we had
just planted.
Unlike the two
National Guard jet
fighters which had
roared us again
and again an hour
earlier, the swallows
were not armed with
four rockets each, and
did not anger me
because I knew
what nation they
guarded, and I sang
aloud to honor them
and their nation.

Song of the Breed

Don't offend
the fullbloods,
don't offend
the whites,
stand there in
the middle
of the god-
damned road
and get hit.

Jim Barnes

Jim Barnes was born in the valley between the San Bois and Kiamichi Mountains in eastern Oklahoma. He is of Choctaw-Welsh descent. In 1951 he migrated to Oregon, where he worked as a lumberjack (river rat and pond monkey) until 1960, at which time he returned to Oklahoma to enter Southeastern Oklahoma State University (B.A., 1964). Later, he earned an M.A. and a Ph.D. in Comparative Literature (English, French, German) from the University of Arkansas. He began writing fiction in the late Fifties and poetry in the Sixties. His first work was published in the Sixties. Since that time his poems, stories, and translations from the French and German have appeared in over 100 magazines, including The Nation, Mundus Artium, Poetry Now, New Letters, The Chicago Review, The Alaska Quarterly Review. *In addition, his poems have appeared in fourteen anthologies, notably* Carriers of the Dream Wheel: Contemporary Native American Poetry *(Harper & Row 1975) and* Heartland II: Poets of the Midwest *(Northern Illinois University Press, 1975). In 1978 he was awarded a national Endowment for the Arts Poetry Fellowship, and in 1980 he received a Translation Prize from the Translation Center of Columbia University—New York for his translation of a volume of German poetry by Dagmar Nick,* Summons and Sign. *He is presently Associate Professor of Comparative Literature at Northeast Missouri State University, where he edits* The Chariton Review, *an international journal of poetry, fiction, and translation.*

Autobiography, Chapter XVII: Floating the Big Piney

How the river cools your blood is something you can't
    explain: you search the bottom stones for words
    unscientific, words fleshed with the sound of sense,
    maybe a chant laid upon the water the time
    words were all and fathers sang their sons ways
    to be and the river flowed sure of its pace.

You lie back in the canoe. Your own child points the bow
    now into the blue breath of sky: trees course
    overhead, and your eyes bend with pillars
    of air, the cornering birds; you lie back into
    the dream you know you'll have just once, a token
    from a far time, a river you can't explain.

All words are lost and you want to sing the meaning
    and origin of things, to make an appositive
    of light, something solid as a stone to hand
    this man-child. But all you have to offer is
    pause, the silence of water and the small
    knowledge that the river takes you over all.

Four Things Choctaw

1.
Nashoba. This my father taught
me how to sing: Wolf, I look long
for you—you know to hide your scrawn-
y hide behind the darkest wind.

2.
Isuba. Horse: not one less than
twenty hands and all fast as hounds
with foxes in their eyes and off.
Chahta isuba cheli. Once
Choctaws bred horses not many
winds could catch. Listen: isuba
still races winter's darkest wind.

3.
Baii. Notice the oak, the high
white bark, the heavy leaves, how they
fall. Winters are long in mountains:
springs freeze at the source and wind bows baii.

4.
Abukbo. The feather that all
my life I sought beyond the sun.
I have fashioned a sacred shaft,
smoothed it red with wet clay and poke.
The feather will guide its arc down
skies where grandfathers walk the woods
quick with game, heavy with the wind's wild mint.

Comcomly's Skull

Concomly's skull is coming home.
That wily one-eyed Chinook chief,
whose other bones are scattered from
the grave, keeper of slaves, thief,
will have his fore-flattened skull
and, gods willing, his fevered soul

back, buried finally and forever,
courtesy Ilwaco, Wash., Cemetery
Association. According to Meriweather,
head of the Chinook Council, "We
plan, for the event, a salmon bake;
we'll call it Chief Comcomly Day."

August 12. Slow birds tread the sun
above the open grave. The priest—
Baptist or Episcopalian,
pagan or seventh son of Crow—casts
a shadow too long for the time
of day. His eulogy turns on rhyme.

After salmon and wine, song birds
and a soft coastal rain begin.
The sun has sunk into the clouds.
Somewhere over against a mountain
a lone wolf lets out one wild howl.
The earnest sky begins to fall.

An unexpected hail. Hell
on dogs and birds. The sky can't hold
its wrath or praise long enough for all
this pomp and circumstance to mold
ancestral flesh onto his skull.
The eyes stay empty. The sky grows full.

Four Choctaw Songs

1. Choctaw Death Song i

When I pass,
this prairie
will hold
my tracks
as long
as the wind
sleeps.

2. Choctaw Death Song ii

I ride
the wind
to another corner
of the sky.

3. Choctaw Hunting Song

Wolf eats
the wind:
his skin
will keep
me warm.

4. Choctaw Eagle Dance Song

Eagle feathers
talk to me:
they say,
touch us to your lips
and know the way
we knew the wind.

Wolf Hunting Near Nashoba*

Nights you wake to sudden stars
and wind that's always on the run.
Hard hills hugging sulphur springs
make echoes leap past your tuning ears.

You turn your collar up and square
your butt into the stone-dead earth
to better feel the oblique sounds at first,
a thirst of bones no mountain waters clear.

The hounds are scaling up the mouths.
The beagle beat is a bit irregular,
but sweet as madrigals in a greening air.
A comet splits the sky from north to south.

You hear yourself yell the bluetick straight
to hell with *go*. Two other dead stars fall.
You count the losing hounds over a hogbacked hill,
eject a cartridge you've lately come to hate.

Times like this you'd like to end it
all. Kill wolf and dogs and shoot the stars.
The thought passes with the chase. At your
feet the fire you forgot you ever lit is out.

---

*Choctaw name for wolf; also the name of a small town in McCurtain County, Oklahoma.

Duane BigEagle

I am of Osage descent (my grandfather was a full blood) born in 1946 at Claremore, Okla. I attended the University of California at Berkeley on a Santa Fe Foundation scholarship. My work has appeared in many magazines and anthologies including: the Chicago Review, Sun Tracks, The Nation, *and* The Remembered Earth *(ed. G. Hobson, Red Earth Press, Albuquerque, 1979). Publications include:* Bidato *(Workingman's Press, Berkeley, 1975) and* Birthplace, Poems & Paintings, *Ten Mile River Press, 1983. Presently I am Statewide Affirmative Action Coordinator for California Poets In The Schools.*

Recollection

How could her dim eyes
have forseen her death
so clearly?
Dark face
color of dry creek beds.
Standing in her yard,
dress held in the wind,
waving a white handkerchief
as we rode away —
"Goodbye grandson, remember me."

Arrows to the heart.

Birthplace

I remember the Indian Hospital
where I was born.
It's built around a courtyard
with a garden and trees in the center.
Years later I would go back
and wait with my mother
in the high ceilinged white walled
reception room
with the dark wooden benches
where people sat.
Through a window across the yard
you could see the maternity ward
and the bush that bloomed
in late spring with fawn yellow flowers.
They say a nurse held me up to that window
the minute I opened my eyes.
I still look for that color —
a fawn yellow glint,
in the eyes of the woman
I'm about to love.

Elegy

A whole tribe dies
with this old man,
he is everyone
waiting bravely.
Sitting there in his handmade
wood and wicker chair
his feet are chilled,
his eyes are about to close.
It's said one enters death
suddenly
without even time to be startled,
or slowly
the way memory fades.
He's certain there's nothing
beyond his last breath.
For an instant
his death song
is like an oak leaf
falling from a tree
on a warm evening
in childhood.

My Grandfather Was A Quantum Physicist

I can see him now
smiling
in full dance costume
with other men
in front of the roundhouse
on a sunny afternoon.

Scientists have finally discovered
that the intimate details
of our lives
are influenced by things
beyond the stars
and beyond time.

My grandfather knew this.

Wind and Impulse

Each moment
rises up screaming into life
born or stillborn.
There are some places
you must not go.
Hate is a stone stairway
to a blank wall.
There are some chances
you cannot pass up.
Love,
a kind of readiness.
The little decisions
make a vision
by which we come to live.
You'd think what you've done
or haven't done
would determine your happiness.
But is that really it?
Does a rabbit
blinded by the headlights of a car
know
if he's going to run
or sit still?
I want to live
like that blinded rabbit,
piercing the darkness
for the slightest
wind and impulse.

Peter Blue Cloud

Peter Blue Cloud (Aroniawenrate) is a Turtle Clan Mohawk from Caughnawaga and a former ironworker. Editor of the Alcatraz Newsletter *in 1969, Poetry Editor of* Akwesasne Notes *from 1975-76. Now living in California, odd-jobbing, wood-carving, writing poetry and stories, he is also one of the editors of* Coyote's Journal.

Books include: ALCATRAZ IS NOT AN ISLAND (Editor), Wingbow Press, 1972; COYOTE & FRIENDS, Blackberry Press, 1976; TURTLE, BEAR & WOLF, Akwesasne Notes Press, 1976; BACK THEN TOMORROW, Blackberry Press, 1978; WHITE CORN SISTER, Strawberry Press, 1979; ELDERBERRY FLUTE SONG, The Crossing Press, 1982.

To-ta Ti-om
(for an aunt)

my aunt was an herb doctor, one-eyed with crooked yellow teeth
    the Christians called her pagan witch
    and their children taunted her
    or ran in fear of their bible lives
        at her approach,
her house of barn lumber leaned into the wind as if toppling
    in winter it grew squat with snow
    and bright sparks from the wood stove
    hissed the snowflakes into steam
        icing the roof,
"when my body dies it will be in winter just in time to see the spring"
    she told this while rolling leaves
    to powder between her boney hands
    for her duty as a medicine person
        was to cure,
in early summer grandfather and i would begin planting
    the corn and beans and squash
    just behind my aunt's house
    and she'd hobble over to help
        plant the tobacco,
as the first green shoots emerged into sunlight
    she would sit on the steps
    grating dried roots into a bowl
    stopping every so often to gaze
        at the garden,
when the time of tobacco curing came she'd be there
    feeling and smelling and tasting
    and every season she would approve
    then later sit by the woodstove
        smoking her pipe,
"Come," she would say to me, "the time for onanoron is here,"
    and she would walk to the pond
    and she would point out strong plants
    for me to wade to and slowly pull
        those medicine roots,
we strung the roots of twisted brown above the woodstove
    to preserve their sacred power
    to be released as needed
    by those who had need
        of such strength,
tiny bundles were made of the roots with bits of string
    then she named the persons
    i was to take onanoron to
    and tied all in a blue bandana
        and said, "go",
this is for Kaienwaktatse and this for Kaerine
    Lives Close to Town
    and She Bends the Boughs
    a penny or two and bread and jam
        I shyly ate,
the pennies slowly filled the glass jar on the table

until my aunt went to the store
a block of salt pork one finger square
a nutmeg, salt and four candies
just for me,
sitting there by the woodstove I would steal a glance
at her tired wrinkled face
and I'd want to shout loud
feeling a tightening in my throat
and maybe cry,
"she was sitting at her table with a bowl in her lap
and it was just turning Spring,"
my grandfather wrote this to me
and i went somewhere to be along
and just sat,
it's planting time again and all done except tobacco
grandfather's leaning on the hoe
and looking at my aunt's house
then he smiles and I smile back
lonely, like crying.

Dogwood Blossoms

It's a question of bright stars
and of four petals cupped
to catch sun and reflect
a hovering circle of white.

Here, where the big trees
were so recently logged-off
and the jagged teeth of stumps
and broken arms of branches
question the meaning of sanity.

a slide of mud and stones
advances down the ravine,
and dogwood and maple are bowed
under weight of future burial.

It's a question of the last act
before man-made dying
that hundreds of blossoms
shout a final triumph
for earth and sky to behold.

Were we to be an armless,
legless race of creatures
belly-crawling thru life
perhaps we could learn of beauty,

but instead we cut down
the very answers we seek
in torn earth, and the secrets
remain unseen by us, as we
plunge forward, blindly,
brushing aside blossoms.

Sweat Song

Coyote
    running
running
    coyote

deserts
    of ice
rivers
    crystal pain
mountains
    breathing
        coyote

sweat bath
    cedar shadow
mirrow hawk
    dream feel
coyote coyote
    obsidian claws
hey, coyote
    hey, coyote

round house
    of coyote
mountains
    breathing
mirror hawk
    hey, coyote
cedar shadow
    hey, coyote

coyote
    running
running
    coyote

song
    done.

Coyote, Coyote, Please Tell Me

What is a shaman?

A shaman I don't know
anything about.
I'm a doctor, myself.
When I use medicine,
it's between me,
my patient,
and the Creation.

    Coyote, Coyote, Please tell me
What is power?

It is said that power
is the ability to start
your chainsaw
with one pull.

    Coyote, Coyote, Please tell me
What is magic?

Magic is the first taste
of ripe strawberries, and
magic is a child dancing
in a summer's rain.

    Coyote, Coyote, please tell me
Why is Creation?

Creation is because I
went to sleep last night
with a full stomach,
and when I woke up
this morning,
everything was here.

    Coyote, Coyote, please tell me
Who you belong to?

According to the latest
survey, there are certain
persons who, in poetic
or scholarly guise,
have claimed me like
a conqueror's prize.

Let me just say
once and for all,
just to be done:
    Coyote,
he belongs to none.

Elderberry Flute Song

He was sitting there on a stone
      at world's end,
all was calm and Creation was
      very beautiful.
There was a harmony and a wholeness
      in dreaming,
and peace was a warming breeze
      given by the sun.

The sea rose and fell
in the rhythm of his mind,
and stars were points of thought
      which led to reason.
The universe turned in the vastness
of space like a dream,
a dream given once and carried
      forever as a memory.

He raised the flute to lips
sweetened by springtime
and slowly played a note
which hung for many seasons
above Creation.
And Creation was content
in the knowledge of music.

The singular note drifted
      far and away
in the mind of Creation,
to become a tiny roundness.
And this roundness stirred
to open newborn eyes
and gazed with wonder
at its own birth.

Then note followed note
in a melody which wove
the fabric of first life.
The sun gave warmth
to waiting seedlings,
and thus were born
the vast multitudes
from the song
      of a flute.

Beth Brant

Born in Detroit May 6, 1941.
Mohawk father.
White mother.
First memory . . .
The harsh shriek of the factory whistle from Ford Motor Co.
The factory hovered over us, turning sheets gray as they
hung to dry.
My eyes stinging from grit and dirt.
Born knowing what "on the line" meant to our lives, our full
or empty stomachs.
The words . . . "laid off" . . . "strike" . . . "organize . . . "union"
First words, first memories.
Second memories . . . .
Grandpa's voice, telling me a story in Mohawk, teaching me
to count, to say special words. Like Grandpa. Grandma.
Smells of corn soup, bubbling and splattering on the cast
iron stove.
Grandma's laughter. The smell of her bodice. Powder and food.
Mama's hands. Sewing clothes. Making quilts. Making do.
Daddy coming home from work. Black hair plastered to his head.
His smell of oil. Of factory. His tender, dirty hand turning
pages of a book he was never too worn out to read to me.
I write what I know, in language that is familiar. I tell
the stories for those who cannot.

for all my Grandmothers

A hairnet covered her head.
a net
encasing the silver strands.
A cage
confining the wildness.
No thread escaped.

(once, your hair coursed down your back
streaming behind
as you ran through the woods.
Catching on branches,
the crackling filaments
gathered leaves.
Burrs attached themselves.
A redbird plucked a shiny thread
for her nest,
shed a feather that glided
into the black cloud and
became a part of you.
You sang as you ran.
Your moccasins
skimmed the earth.
Heh ho oh heh heh)

Prematurely taken
from the woodland.
Giving birth
to children that grew
in a world that is white.
Prematurely
you put your hair up and
covered it
with a net.
Prematurely grey
they called it.

Hair Binding.

Damming the flow.

With no words, quietly
the hair fell out
formed webs on your dresser
on your pillow
in your brush.
These tangles strands
pushed to the back of a drawer
wait for me.
To untangle
To comb through
To weave together the split fibers
and make a material
Strong enough
to encompass our lives.

Ride the Turtle's Back

A woman grows hard and skinny.
She squeezes into small corners.
Her quick eyes uncover dust and cobwebs.
She reaches out
for flint and sparks fly in the air.
Flames turned loose on fields
burn down to the bare seeds
we planted deep.

The corn is white and sweet.
Under its pale, perfect kernels
a rotting cob is betrayal
and it lies in our bloated stomachs.

I lie in Grandmother's bed
and dream the earth into a turtle.
She carries us slowly across the universe.
The sun warms us.
At night the stars do tricks.
The moon caresses us.

We are listening for the sounds of food.

Mother is giving birth, Grandmother says.
Corn whispers.
The earth groans with labor
turning corn yellow in the sun.

I lie in Grandmother's bed.

We listen.

We listen.

Native Origin

The old women are gathered in the Longhouse. First, the ritual kissing on the cheeks, the eyes, the lips, the top of the head; that spot where the hair parts in the middle like a wild river through a canyon. On either side, white hair flows unchecked, unbinded.

One Grandmother sets the pot over the fire that has never gone out. To let the flames die is a taboo, a breaking of trust. The acorn shells had been roasted the night before. Grandmother pours the boiling water over the shells. An aroma rises and combines with the smell of wood smoke, sweat, and the sharp, sweet odor of blood.

The acorn coffee steeps and grows dark and strong. The old women sit patiently in a circle, not speaking. Each set of eyes stares sharply into the air, or into the fire. Occasionally, a sigh escapes from an open mouth. A Grandmother has a twitch in the corner of her eye. She rubs her nose, then smooths her hair.

The coffee is ready. Cups are brought out of a wooden cupboard. Each woman is given the steaming brew. They blow on the swirling liquid, then slurp the drink into their hungry mouths. It tastes good. Hot, strong, dark. A little bitter, but that is all to the good.

The women begin talking among themselves. They are together to perform a ceremony. Rituals of women take time. There is no hurry.

The magic things are brought out from pockets and pouches.

A turtle rattle made from a she-turtle who was a companion of the women's mother. It died the night she died, both of them ancient and tough. Now, the daughter shakes the rattle, and mother and she-turtle live again. Another Grandmother pulls out a bundle that contains a feather from a hermit thrush. This is a holy feather. Of all the birds in the sky, hermit thrush is the only one who flew to the Spirit World. It was there she learned her beautiful song. She is clever and hides from sight. To have her feather is great magic. The women pass around the feather. They tickle each other's chins and ears. Giggles and laughs erupt in the dwelling.

From that same bundle of the hermit thrush, come kernels of corn, yellow, red, black. They rest in her wrinkled, dry palm. These are also passed around. Each woman holds the corn in her hand for a while before giving it to her sister. Next come the leaves of Witch Hazel and Jewelweed. Dandelion roots for chewing, Pearly Everlasting for smoking. These things are given careful consideration, and much talk is generated over the old ways of preparing the concoctions.

A woman gives a smile and brings out a cradleboard from behind her back. There is nodding of heads and smiling and long drawn-out ahhhs. The cradleboard has a beaded back that a mother made in her ninth month. An old woman starts a song; the rest join in:

Little baby
Little baby
Ride on Mother's back
Laugh, laugh
Life is good
Mother shields you

A Grandmother wipes her eyes, another holds her hands and kisses the lifelines. Inside the cradleboard are bunches of moss taken from a menstrual house. This moss has staunched rivers of blood that generations of young girls have squeezed from their wombs.

The acorn drink is reheated and passed around again. A woman adds wood to the fire. She holds her hands out to the flames. It takes a lot of heat to warm her creaky body. Another woman comes behind her with a warm blanket. She wraps it around her friend and hugs her shoulders. They stand quietly before the fire.

A pelt of fur is brought forth. It once belonged to a beaver. She was found one morning, frozen in the ice, her lodge unfinished. The beaver was thawed and skinned. The women worked the hide until it was soft and pliant. It was the right size to wrap a new born baby in, or to comfort old women on cold nights.

A piece of flint, an eagle bone whistle, a hank of black hair, cut in mourning; these are examined with reverant vibrations.

The oldest Grandmother removes her pouch from around her neck. She opens it with rusty fingers. She spreads the contents in her lap. A fistful of black earth. It smells clean, fecund. The women inhale the odor, the metallic taste of iron is on their tongues, like sting.

The oldest Grandmother scoops the earth back into her pouch. She tugs at the strings, it closes. The pouch lies between her breasts, warming her skin. Her breasts are supple and soft for one so old. Not long ago, she nursed a sister back to health. A child drank from her breast and was healed of evil spirits that entered her while she lay innocent and dreaming.

The ceremony is over. The magic things are put in their places. The old women kiss and touch each other's faces. They go out in the night. The moon and stars are parts of the body of Sky Woman. She glows on, never dimming. Never receding.

The Grandmothers go inside the Longhouse. They tend the fire, and wait.

Photo by W. Paul Smith

Diane Burns

Diane Burns is Anishinabe (Ojibwa), and Chemehuevi Indian, and attended the Institute of American Indian Art in Sante Fe, New Mexico where she was awarded the Congressional Medal of Merit for academic and artistic excellence. She later attended Barnard College of Columbia University in New York City. Her first book of poetry, RIDING THE ONE-EYED FORD, 1981, has been nominated for the William Carlos Williams Award, and is included in the St. Marks Poetry Project's "Ten Best of the Year." Her poetry has appeared in magazines and journals such as The Greenfield Review, Sunbury, White Pine Journal, New York Waterways, Hard Press, and Contact/II. She is a painter and illustrator and has written book reviews for the Council on Inter-racial Books for Children. She is a member of the Poet's Overland Expeditionary Troop (POET), which has brought poetry to life in theatrical settings in galleries and schools across the country, and a member of the Third World Writers Association and the Feminist Writers Guild. Maureen Owen writes of her, "She's not here to make you comfortable ... she crosses cultures like most people cross a street in New York ... against the light, into full traffic with the grace that makes your eyes water."

Our People

Our people
slit open the badger
to see the tomorrows
in its blood.

Now
look at me
and see what our
tomorrows hold.

We lie together
Souls slit open raw
         and bleeding

We embrace
And rub
      the wounds
          together.

Gadoshkibos

Gadoshkibos
the warrior
He would sign no treaties
"Foolish" he called them
The whites are crazy
The whites are crazy
they sang around the fires at night
when the Anishinabe knew the trappers were gone.

Gadoshkibos
great grandfather
dies in ecstacy
Nakota arrow in his throat, cries
The whites are crazy
Why fight among each other when we know?
The real enemy rushes us like buffaloes into a trap.

Gadoshkibos
son of the same
lays at night with his wives.
They ran, hid, but now
they stay put year round.
The whites are crazy.
The children starve on commodity food
and he wonders where the Anishinabe warriors have gone.

Gadoshkibos
wife, the second,
struggles with her garden
ground is good with blood
spilled there and she knows
the whites are crazy
and she handles her hoe like a rifle.
Her sisters in the nations watch the children and know they must wait.

Gadoskibos
the latest one
reads sociology
at Pomona State
and studies just why
the whites are crazy.
Summertimes he goes back to the blanket
and he wanders the woods and wonders where the warriors have gone.

Big Fun

I don't care if you're married I still love you
I don't care if you're married
After the party's over
I will take you home in my One-Eyed Ford
Way   yah hi yo, Way yah hi yo!

  Modene!
  the roller derby queen!
  She's Anishinabe,
  that means Human Being!
That's H for hungry!
and B for frijoles!
          frybread!
          Tortillas!
          Watermelon!
          Pomona!
Take a sip of this
and a drag of that!
At the rancheria fiesta
It's tit for tat!
Low riders and Levis
go fist in glove!
Give it a little pat
a push or a shove
Move it or lose it!
Talk straight or bruise it!
Everyone
has her fun
when the sun
is all done
We're all one
make a run
hide your gun
Hey!
I'm no nun!
'49 in the hills above
          Ventura
Them Okies gotta drum

I'm from Oklahoma
I got no one to call my own
if you will be my honey
I will be your sugar pie, way hi yah,
Way yah hey way yah hi yah!

We're gonna sing all night
bring your blanket
or
be that way then!

DOA in Dulse

He fell off the wheel of souls
after WWII
alarmed at the lights in the hospital
promptly punched a giant nurse
& continued in the same vein
for quite some time.

It was his blessing & his downfall
to be the son of Indian parents
He learned of hunger to his new body
and the peaceful glow a beer brings

He might have been Geronimo
in his past lives
or Sakajaweiah
or a berdache healer

He grew up fighting
punching big nurses at every turn
Orating at length on solutions
& ways to deaden the Red People's pain.

But he needed the Red People to listen
When they didn't he deadened his own.
He knew how, these ways needed only
Time to work, a supply and money
and they worked every time.

In 1978
  When he was twenty-one
a big nurse wheeled his remains somewhere
while he joined the wheel again
          for another
                    crack at all.

Sure You Can Ask Me A Personal Question

How do you do?
    No, I am not Chinese.
No, not Spanish.
    No, I am American Indi--uh, Native American.
No, not from India.
    No, not Apache.
No, not Navajo.
    No, not Sioux.
No, we are not extinct.
    Yes, Indin.
Oh?
    So that's where you got those high cheekbones.
Your great grandmother, huh?
    An Indian Princess, huh?
Hair down to there?
    Let me guess. Cherokee?
Oh, so you've had an Indian friend?
    That close?
Oh, so you've had an Indian lover?
    That tight?
Oh, so you've had an Indian servant?
    That much?
Yeah, it was awful what you guys did to us.
    It's real decent of you to apologize.
No, I don't know where you can get peyote.
    No, I don't know where you can get Navajo rugs real cheap.
No, I didn't make this. I bought it at Bloomingdales.
    Thank you. I like your hair too.
I don't know if anyone knows whether or not Cher is really Indian.
    No, I didn't make it rain tonight.
Yeah. Uh-huh. Spirituality.
    Uh-huh. Yeah. Spirituality. Uh-huh. Mother
Earth. Yeah. Uh'huh. Uh-huh. Spirituality.
    No, I didn't major in archery.
Yeah, a lot of us drink too much.
    Some of us can't drink enough.
This ain't no stoic look.
    This is my face.

Barney Bush

August was nearly over. Snakes were regaining their eyesight after this moon of blindness, the legends say. The banks of the Ohio River were silent as the water slowly merged with the Mississippi about thirty miles downstream. Hot summer clouds lay plastered to the humid sky, and Europeans and Euroamericans were winding down from their second world war. I was cut from my mother's sweat during these times. I don't remember the fiery blood sun hovering over the west or the stillness. They say I cried for the first time when the hawk screamed over the house. It must have been then that I recall the sounds of the cicadas.

Sometimes I think of all the recent lives I've been a part of and find it hard to believe that my childhood is part of my present lifetime. I remember grandparents and great grandparents, who remembered their great grandparents and stories back to when our muddy flesh first oozed through our Creator's fingers. And that mud was in this land called North America.

I left home at sixteen to travel all over the United States, northern Mexico and Canada. During these hitchhiking days, I took time to study art at the Institute of American Indian Arts in Santa Fe, New Mexico, and finish a degree in the humanities at Ft. Lewis College, Durango, Colorado, in 1972. In 1978, I went to Idaho and completed a Master's Degree in English and Fine Arts at the universtiy in Moscow. The intensities involving all these years are forthcoming in novel form sometime in 1983.

May it be that we all learn to walk in balance and in beauty with this, our mother the earth, and our creator.

Blood

for Richard Emerson Jack

Turning deer flesh over
the hot fire   turning
my face from the oak
smoke   I smelled you
You are almost here
        Ahneen Neegi
Where do you sit tonight
I am smiling for you
Coyotes wail at bottom of
the bluff   and here a
sacred glow   my own blood
where there are
blessings in every wind
In the fire   my
transfixed eyes flicker
inviolably   wanting to
see you in the gentle
light   holy way in our
blood   terrestrial blood
our way that others presume
The meat is roasted   blood
to be devoured by humid
summer breezes or
winds that bite with
teeth of winter ice.

It Is Finished

The dreams are old before you
say them   round around
round   and
moons silent figure attracts
your whisper
Humanitys dark bell thunders
loudly   in bellies that
hunger for war
I sit here with you in this
dream   this photograph among
my mothers sons   this
campsmoke
this moment   another time
already lived
What crying night wind does
your soulful eyes release
like an invisible lariat to

hold me at a manitos edge
When we are alone   alone
our words are cedar boughs
bending   but my
Shawnee voice cracks   when
we divide
Within the circle we
sing   harmony revolving
in all directions   like
the spirit of blue light that
pours from our mouths
spirit within spirit   once
broken from the circle
wanders aimlessly   until
we dream
dreams inside dreams.

Whose Voice

My father taught
me the sound of
screech owl   Semyalwa
late fall evenings
when aroma of wood
smoke seared lungs and
watered eyes
He would peep around
trees at me   a
crazy face   making
the owls sound   when
purple thistle and
golden rods alter the
skys vision   when
our land was frosted
shadows that thawed
the stories of
grandparents
Semyalwas voice yet
startles me   where
the road breaks   when
I think I am
alone   and I will
still shiver.

Voice In The Blood

Outside
yellow leaves rattle
My eyes squint between
realities   all those
relatives in my
dreams   and fields of
dark antlered clouds
rationing sunlight into
shadows beside my bed
Wind sounds like it
should be cold   like
there should be geese
the ones who snatched
up my great grandmothers
ghost   that quiet
childhood time when I
was watching
I was alone with her
didnt know what I was
supposed to do to
stop them
Beneath her star blanket
she told me in words as
old as this earth   not
to listen
I told her it was too
late
She wanted to protect the
blood   the silence that
she left me   as she
went south over amber
hills
as grandmothers do every
fall   knowing they
have grandchildren   half
behind   half
with them.

Another Old Song

Medicine plants blooming beneath
dogwood   redbud
edged our sad footsteps from
singing creek hollow   like
your own departure   "see you later"
Road west of Quapaw
you this time   a new flute melody
in cerulean air playing from my
pores   memory from unreal
lifetimes   ancient hills
stories   gravel road and
buzzards circling
this memory   real or not
wanting your human smell to
stay on my breath
One hundred fifty miles gone by
now   your face in sun glaring
truck glass   singing   watching
sorting out feelings into visions
wondering if "summer's end" will
be meaningless by then
By your home fire   don't make
me into a story for your grandchildren
you looking into flames   wondering
what it would have really
been like.

Gladys Cardiff

My father was from the Owl family in Cherokee, North Carolina, and my mother is predominantly Irish and Welsh. I was born in Browning, Montana in 1942 where my parents were principal and music teacher on the Blackfoot reservation.

I arrived in Seattle as an infant in a laundry basket in the back seat of our Chevy. I grew up in an upper middleclass neighborhood. My father, having experienced racial prejudice in his career with the Indian service had our name changed to Harris at this time. I have experienced the ambivalence of great pride in my Native American heritage with estrangement from any close association with my people from this background. Throughout my father's lifetime he did research on the Cherokees and both parents recounted stories and recollections. My mother is a musician and composer, and through her influence I have been exposed to the arts. My father was one of the first to leave the reservation and achieve a Masters degree. He has instilled in me a continuation and desire to preserve the history of the Cherokees.

One of the sacred formulas of the Cherokees includes this phrase. "Let the paths from every direction recognize each other". It is a blessing and a prayer, and to me it is especially poignant. In relation to poetry it suggests a special type of knowing. The sort of associative imagining where resonances are caught from every direction, rational, sensual, metaphysical, and meet in a poem in specific details and texture and form—all aspects joined in an act of resolution and revelation—this is a wonderful recognition. Writing, for me, is an act of affirmation and celebration.

Long Person

Dark as wells, his eyes
Tell nothing. They look
Out from the print with small regard
For this occasion.
Dressed in neat black, he sits
On a folded newspaper
On a sawhorse in front of his blacksmith shop.
Wearing a black suit and white, round-brimmed hat,
My father stands on one side, his boy face
Round and serious. His brother stands
Like a reflection on the other side.
They each hold a light grasp on the edge
Of their daddy's shoulder, their fingernails
Gleaming like tiny moons on the black wool.
Each points his thumb up at the sky,
As if holding him too closely, with their whole hand,
Would spur those eyes into statement.
Coming out of a depth known as dream—
Or is it memory?
I can see inside the door where the dim shapes
Of bellows and tongs, rings and ropes hang on the wall,
The place for fire, the floating anvil,
Snakes of railroad steel, wheels in heaps,
Piled like turtles in the dark corners.
Oconoluftee, Long Person,
You passed a stone's throw away from his door,
Your ripples are Cherokee prayers.
River, Grandfather,
May your channels never break.

To Frighten A Storm

O now you come in rut,
in rank and black desire
to beat the brush, to lash
the wind with your long hair.
Ha! I am afraid,
Exceedingly afraid.
But see? her path goes there,
along the swaying tops
of trees, up to the hills.
Too long she is alone.
Bypass our fields, and mount
your ravages of fire
and rain on higher trails.
You shall have her lying down
upon the smoking mountains.

Tlanusi' Yi, The Leech Place

Surely it is death to come here.
This rock overhang
opens a shadowy well in the river
to give me a deep look.
I am hungry for fish.
I forget the woman tossed up
downstream,
her face without nose or ears.
I never saw
the baby that disappeared,
the quiet sleeper.
"I'll tie red leech skins upon my legs
and wear them for garters".
My song scythes over wet fields
parting the water like braids
wound with foam feathers,
wound with sunperches, snakes, and green turtles.
"I'll tie red leech skins upon my legs
and wear them for garters."
Its breath is like milk.
Young as I am, I am
old in a striped ahunwogi,
girdled in red and in water,
Young as I am I know
the secret caverns of the Hiwassee,
that the river is eating the land.
I was hungry for fish.
I was from Birdtown.
I am dressed in a whirlpool of leech skins.
I am no more.

Combing

Bending, I bow my head
And lay my hand upon
Her hair, combing, and think
How women do this for
Each other. My daughter's hair
Curls against the comb,
Wet and fragrant—orange
Parings. Her face, downcast,
Is quiet for one so young.

I take her place. Beneath
My mother's hands I feel
The braids drawn up tight
As a piano wire and singing,
Vinegar-rinsed. Sitting
Before the oven I hear
The orange coils tick
The early hour before school.

She combed her grandmother
Mathilda's hair using
A comb made out of bone.
Mathilda rocked her oak wood
Chair, her face downcast,
Intent on tearing rags
In strips to braid a cotton
Rug from bits of orange
and brown. A simple act,

Preparing hair. Something
Women do for each other,
Plaiting the generations.

Owl And Rooster

Gatigwanasti, Ayunini, Suate,
Tsa lagi names,
I place them on my tongue,
chew them like reeds or hide.
Deep in the ravine coyote wakes,
his high staccato bark
punctuates the alarms of distant sirens.

    Grandfather and Great-grandfather walk together
    through the Darkening Land.
    They hear Wahuhu cry his warning.

Tsistege-uska, tsistege-uska,
the cat wraps his feathery engine
around a dream of rat's heads.
The children sleep in another room.

Kuwahi, Echota, Hiwassee,
Wolftown, the Mulberry Place,
I weave a basket shaped
leaf on reed, reed on hide,
a cavern of ribs to hold these names
that move my voice
until it pours like water.

    Wahuhu, wahuhu.
    Owl cries outside government walls.
    Spring Peeper and Standing Deer awake.
    Their tongues dry in their mouths
    like tomahawk leather lashed around stone.

Below my window the rosecomb rooster
mounts the maple,
heralds the long coo-coo-ree arc into morning.
The ghosts in ahunwogis
become trees again,
the Ancient One pulls
his fine, blue knitting of smoke skyward.
Birds rain into my breakfast cup.
Soon I must wake the children for school.
Now as they sleep
the sound of their breathing
is the rustle of willow and wings,
the shuf, shuf of moccasins
worn by old men
dancing around ghost fires.
Someday I will show them this basket
filled with water
that sings.

Self portrait

Robert J. Conley

Robert J. Conley, Director of Indian Studies at Morningside College in Sioux City, Iowa, was born in Oklahoma in 1940. He is an enrolled tribal member of the United Keetoowah Band of Cherokee Indians in Oklahoma. Prior to his position in Iowa, he was Assistant Programs Director for the Cherokee Nation of Oklahoma, Director of Indian Studies at Bacone College, Coordinator of Indian Culture at Eastern Montana College, and Instructor of English at Southwest Missouri State University and at Northern Illinois University. A member of Western Writers of America, Conley's poems and stories, most of which deal with his Cherokee background have been published in numerous magazines and anthologies. He is the author of 21 Poems *(Aux Arcs Press) and* Adawosgi, Swimmer Wesley Snell: A Cherokee Memorial *(The Blue Cloud Quarterly Press).*

untitled

I am not a shaman
and my poems are not magic.
how can I presume
by scratching out my thoughts
by this small act
how can I or anyone presume
to claim the knowledge
and the power that's gained
by years of study
and by fasting sacrifice
and from holy visions?
If I believe in sin
then such a claim to me is sin.

Language is sacred
a gift from God
and its misuse is sinful.

A poem should be honest.

A man who tries a poem should be humble.

My poem might be a prayer
and offering or a joke
and it is sacred
only insofar as it is honest—
no more—no less.

Tom Starr

They say Tom Starr
all by himself
rubbed out 100 men.

They say he hid
from laws
one time inside a cave
and lay so long
and still
he watched a spider
spin a web
to seal the entrance.

And then they say
the laws came by
and saw the cave
but when they saw the web

they said, "No need
to look in there. No one
has gone in there for quite some time."

And when he died
at home
in bed
at peace
his hair had all turned white.

Ned Christie

He cooked cornbread
(mixed in the meal pounded dried squirrel)
in a huge pot:
a fire on the lid.

He was marble champion (unofficial)
of the Cherokee Nation.

They say the boys came
from miles around
to shoot for his marbles
to eat his delicious cornbread.

He was a blacksmith
a gunsmith
a legislator.

They said (the whites)
he was an outlaw.

23 men
a cannon
and dynamite
in 1892

killed him
displayed his body on a slab

posed with it
for their photograph
(something to leave their children & their children's children).

In a cemetery
where now hogs root
lie the bones of *Nede Wade.*

On the marker
now knocked down
is told

he was a blacksmith
and was
a brave
man.

Wili Woyi, Shaman, also known as Billy Pigeon

While U.S. marshals
searched the woods
for Billy Pigeon

Wili Woyi
sat & watched
his Soul
in the body of an owl.

Sometimes
invisible
he walked among them.

The marshals
being white
& having no belief

never caught him

and never

understood.

The Hills of *Tsa la gi*

for Gene LeRoy Hart

They framed him once
and put him in their jail,
and he escaped
and stayed hid out three years
with family and friends
never really leaving home.
And then they framed him once again—
the second for a heinous crime.
And then began (they say)
the most intensive manhunt
in the history of the state.
They searched the woods.
Two bloodhounds died.
And Hart endured it ten more months
before they got him.

A Cherokee can disappear from white men's eyes
in the wooded hills of Oklahoma.
Ned Christie hid out seven years.
Billy Pigeon holds the record at eleven
(and then they never really got him).

These hills are Cherokee,
and Cherokees slip into their brambles and their brush
like a fish glides through a stream.
The *yonegs* enter as invading forces
and hack and stomp and burn their way.

They say that long ago
a boy so liked the woods,
he took his family to live out there,
and they became the bears.
That boy was Cherokee.

I thank these hills for what they've done.
I thank them for their welcome.
I hurt for them
when white men cut their trees
or burn them up
or fence them off.
I pray that they'll endure.
I pray that Hart escapes again
and finds himself once more
in the safety of the hills of *Tsa la gi*.

The Rattlesnake Band

"don't wear that snake
for a hatband, boy,
you'll get struck by lightnin', sure."

     In the house of thunder,
     Thunder's Son, the Lightning Boy,
     wound a rattlesnake round his neck
     to make a pretty necklace.

he walked with a swagger
& when he did, the rattles would sound.
ignore old superstitious men. be cool.

     The Lightning Boy
     flashed here and there
     around the ballfield—
     played circles all around
     his brothers—
     outnumbered two to one
     he won the game.

     There was once a time
     a hunter in the woods
     found himself surrounded
     by rattlesnakes
     the Chief—a very large one—spoke.
     "Your wife," it said, "just now
     has killed my brother.
     when you go home," it said,
     "make her go outside for water.
     And I will kill her."
     The hunter, though he loved his wife,
     did what the rattler said,
     and she was killed.

At the carwash
the boy with the rattlesnake band
was washing his car
when Lightning struck
the metal roof overhead

     One time in Cherokee country
     Lightning struck a house.
     a family of six
     lies cold in a single grave
     their names are listed there.
     "Killed by Lightning," it says.

On a shelf in the house
the hat with the rattlesnake band
is gathering dust.

Charlotte DeClue

Born July 9, 1948 in Enid, Oklahoma. Graduated from highschool in Oklahoma City. Attended Oklahoma State University in Stillwater, and the University of Missouri-Kansas City. Have been writing for about five years.
Currently living in Lawrence, Kansas with my husband and teenage son.

Morning Song.

Grey is the color of time
when all things stretch
in the four directions
and nothing is touched
with defeat.

Niki nonk'on
Owononk'on ieh
Dawn is the child
wet with birth.
Owononk'on ieh
Sky pulls its sheets back
and nurses the clouds,
tickles their bellies,
and they run.
And the sun warms the feathers
of the washinga.
Earth-maker reminds us
things are not the same.
Niki wathon
Song goes out
across the space
between night and day
telling us
we have slept
while the spirits walked
the earth.
Niki wathon
Niki nonk'on
And oh,
what is it to be awakened from life.

Yesterday, Robin spoke to me.
My hands were tied, twisted together
with strings of gut,
loosened with sweat, and dried with sleep.
And yet I could hear,
but the words twisted my hands tighter.
And she spoke and laughed at me,
and danced in the pale, watery air.
Can you free my hands, I asked her.
And they dropped to my lap,
my fingers separating.
I counted them, wein ... thonba ... thabathin ...
while she sat
balanced in the wind.
Who has come to play with me, I asked.
Is it you?
The branch snapped.
Winter's heart, you will not make it
through the spring, she cried.
I will catch you, ShinKu KuGe,
I said. I will catch you and cut your heart out.

Today, Robin barely lifts herself
from the ground.
I watch her,
my arms falling lightly to my side
circling 'round my back, spreading
gently in the wind.

Tomorrow,
she will die.

Place-Of-Many-Swans.

I sit on the ground
in the path of the little spider, Tsechobe.
Like the great grey fish,
the clouds dip their heads
in their watery sky.
When the sun leaves unnoticed
and hints of daylight for someone else,
the poet waits for the moon.
But i am somewhere in between
making the shadows my friends,
giving them faces i have seen before,
ancient and wise,
and crying.

The people that lived here
came from the trees
and were proud in the way they stood.
But they were whittled away,
first their limbs,
then their center,
and left bare.

Tsechobe walks across my feet
and darts in and out of the shadows.
I think she limps
from an old wound.
Are you lonely without them, Tsechobe?
Will you cry when I leave?

Who weeps over fallen trees?

In Memory of the Moon. (A Killing.)

the hated dog sits
in the blackest part of the night
where the edges of earth will never turn to day.
his eyes are red, for they see only the Moon
and the blood.

he slept alone
under the tables and between the stools
licking his hunter's boots,
thinking about the afternoon sun chasing him
through the open door.
it made him angry.

the Moon walked out of her house and down an empty road.
and the hated dog
with the taste of his master's boots in his mouth,
followed her.

and the sun fell to its knees
and buffed the sky with a bloody haze.
the wind blew once more warm, then cold.

the hated dog killed the Moon.

Ijajee's Story.

When you are traveling
and find yourself alone,
it is not wise
to think of yourself as ignorant.
Because when you travel alone
you have no one to depend on
but yourself.
And would you trust someone
you thought to be ignorant?

Just say, "I do not understand."
These things that you do not
understand . . . . .
put them into a bag
and carry them over your shoulder.
As time goes on,
the bag will get empty.

To the spirit of Monahsetah
and to all women who have been
forced to the ground.

(from the banks of the Konce.)

there is death in this river
you can hear it speak.

the people fishing
or watching the great birds
nest in shallow coves
cannot hear it.
they have not been made to listen.

i have seen the eagles
and cast for fish

but there is something else here.
the Mystery that speaks
of life and death
and rebirth
has been stretched to its limits.
violence has imposed
new conditions.

if i could
i would pull the death from this river.
if i could
i would fling it to the sky.
but today the clouds hang
bruised and battered
as if saying
they too have had enough.

for downstream
a woman's body was found

delivered naked and nameless
into the river's lap.

my fingers claw wet clay
        touch earth touch earth.
if you get lost
        touch earth.
if the wind changes directions
or you are caught midstream
        touch earth.

when violence hits you
        touch deep
for that is where it strikes.
the place
the moment
when the killer and his instrument
become one.

cold lifeless metal
held to my throat.
hand digging into pain.

i close my eyes to push
back the memory
but there is no stopping it.
no force of mind
no threat of retaliation.
(victims are stripped of will.)

only the sheer nothingness
of a star breaking
into a million pieces
falling scattering.
and the sound
that only those who have heard
a star fall
can hear.

if i could
i would heal you Ushuaka
Woman's-self.
and we would walk again
without fear
without stumbling.

we would walk together
you and i
and talk about this and that.
(but not about what we have in common.)
we would forget
and the river would be as it once was.

      at night
      the river flows silently
      past my bed
      while the full moon
      echoes across my floor

        be whole again
        little one.
        be whole.

Anita Endrezze-Danielson

I live in Greenbluff, Washington (about 20 miles north of Spokane) in the middle of a large forest. My husband, Dave, and my 2½ year old son, Aaron, and I live in a log house we are slowly building ourselves. I don't have "an outside job". I work in cycles on my poetry, seeming to write the most from Spring to Fall.

I like poems that are rich in imagery. I usually write about nature, mainly because I'm literally immersed in it, but lately I'm trying to get more people in my poems too.

I have a Master of Arts degree from Eastern Washington University in Creative Writing. I have taught high school and college English in the past as well as being poet in residence for the local school district for 2 years.

Chapbooks: Burning the Fields, Confluence Press, 1983 *and* The North People, *Blue Cloud Quarterly, 1983.*

Why Stone Does Not Sing By Itself

It is the foundation for all other songs.

If you hold a blue rock to your ear,
you will hear the ancient river
that kept it as its heart,
the dry wind that used it for its tongue,
and the earth that promised it a mouth of fire.

A speckled rock is from the dream
of a galloping appaloosa.
The herd sings its Ceremony of Grass
and their dream-stones fly from their hooves
into the spattered sky.

A black rock has the bear's soul caught
in his last sleep. His song circles
the stone, giving it the illusion
of fur.

All yellow rocks keep the secrets of Owls.
All green rocks are the breaths of plants
singing in nightly joy.

A red fist-sized rock is the love
of a man and a woman as their bodies sing
on the grass.

A gray stone is naturally mournful.
It is a word from the common language of the dead.
Keep it. Someday you will understand.

Night Mare

Collision: two seconds before, I saw the dark
chest of the horse, muscles gleaming in the rain,
silhouetted in the headlights of an on-coming truck.
Then the glass shattered into slivers and globules,
some shaped like startled birds or teeth-like flowers,
others just thin and sharp as a nightjar's cry.
"A horse ran into our car," I said shocked, quiet
as a prayer. My young son repeats "I'm so lucky
to be alive." He is reassured by my breathing,
by the trees bending, the storm ignoring our relief.
We get out, my husband shaking glass shards
from his shirt. Two white horses quiver
under the trees, rolling their white-rimmed eyes,
rain darkening their nostrils and lips
until it seems as if they are breathing the night.
But it's the black horse that bolted down the road;
her sides heave as we try to calm her, whispering
it's alright, it's alright. Her hooves are sleek
but blunted: they leave strange tracks in the mud,
shining like glass wings, curved and half-open.
There is blood under the hooves of the dark horse—
she stares over our shoulders, dreaming of the ancient
language of horses: wide-mouthed, sweet-appled, breathless.
She shivers, waiting for her True Master to take her
into more familiar pastures, to comb her down
with tufts of grass by the old barn with its chickens
laying eggs on pale straw, and where the barn owl
roosts with the hens in the coldest winters,
the moon glimmering like a salt-lick. Dark Horse,
are you longing for the wind to braid your mane
into wild songs and for the spring rains to flood
the field remembering your great hunger
for the sun growing vertical and green? Dark Horse,
you are almost darker than this sinewy dark.
You are almost faster than the wind in your memories.
Our low voices murmur distantly, like the promise
of cool water at the end of a long journey.
It's alright. You're almost there.

There Are Three Bones in The Human Ear

One hears Light harnessing the strong back of the sky-ox,
the steady creak of the moon as it wheels on its thin rim,
the sigh of his wife as she sows star-grains that will bloom
for centuries in the dark fields. Some grains drift slowly
into your eyes and for awhile every man is a god.

*

One hears the family of Death, unexpectedly arriving
for a long stay. There is the brother made of rain,
whose face is always grey and nothing more.
There is the sister made of ferns; her face is hidden
but you know her eyes are white and pupil-less.
Ash is the mother's voice. Or dust.
She remembers your grandmother's death
as if it were her own. The father is trying
to express his regrets but the words fall like powder
from his lips. Nothing you say or do
will make them leave.
They'll eat your food until your fingers
are extensions of air.
They'll drink your water until your tongue feels like a bone.
They'll take your name, and through misuse
or no use at all, let it harden to stone.

*

The third bone, hearing the voice of Love
somewhere just out of reach,
sounds so familiar you turn—startled—and call:
wait for me.

Blue Horses: West Winds

Across a pasture of yellow lillies,
the blue horses race:
fetlocks steel-blue,
bellies reflecting the green-blue of new grass,
broad backs sky-blue,
chests colored dark indigo like storm clouds,
eyes like points of midnight,
tails washed in rain, grey-blue and pearly.

The wind is a dialect
felt on the muzzle.
It brings back memories of the First Birth
on a grassy shore, horses tumbling
out of the foam like lost shells,
their manes hardening from mist
to filaments of sea-rough hair,
their cries becoming more than spray
but always salty.

Who has heard a horse sing?
It is a song of longing
in a long throat
and pure as wind on water.
These blue horses are far
from the sea; they live on air.

Under a cottonwood, I call:
come to me! They are waiting
for the Horse-Goddess to stamp her hooves
in the clouds overhead.
Their tongues taste light.
They hum an old chant, thrumming
the words deep into the earth:
Daughters of Diaphanous Waters, sons of Zephyr!

They want to become water again,
to believe in the strong muscle of the SeaHeart,
to touch the tiny horses that sway on their tails
like green charms, to know only the weight
of a salt-brimmed moon on their backs.
Their wild running is a letting go.
I am weak and remain tethered to this land.
I have no choice. They disappear
into the mouse-eared willows,
their blue tails as whip-sharp as a March wind.

Song-Maker

There is a drunk on Main Avenue, slumped
in front of the Union Gospel Mission.
He is dreaming of pintos the color of wine
and ice, and drums that speak the names
of wind. His hair hides his face,
but I think I know him.

Didn't he make songs people still sing
in their sleep?
Didn't coyotes beg him for new songs
to give to the moon?
Didn't he dance all night once and laugh
when the women suddenly turned
shy at dawn?
Didn't he make a song just for me,
one blessed by its being sung only once?

If he would lift his face
I could see his eyes, see
if he's singing now
a soul-dissolving song.
But he's all hunched over
and everyone walks around him.
He must still have strong magic
to be so invisible.

I remember him saying:
Even grass has a song,
'though only wind hears it.

Self portrait

Nia Francisco

Borne to the Salt clan and mothered by the Red Button clan ... I am Nia Francisco.

It is said that a person knows the self if one knows the clans or "the people" one belongs to. My father's mother and father took me into their home as a new born babe. They raised me until I was twelve years old. At that time I returned to my natural parents. Navajo language is my first language. A language I think of as the mother of my thoughts and dreams.

In 1969, a group of strange new people determined what would happen to my direction in life. I don't attribute every decision or change in my life to them, I did most of the work—but at this time they gave human love, and sincere concern for the oppressed. These people were Volunteers in Service to America (VISTA) workers of the Office of Economic Opportunity—a federally funded program. These people became friends—yet very threatening to me, the way I was and my community; Shiprock, NM. They promoted and advocated honesty to self, self-dignity, self-respect, worthiness, self-love and accountability for one's own acts and many human acts. In that period and time too many of us Navajo people were always subjected to suppression by well-educated and wealthier people—especially white Americans living amongst us. The way VISTA workers help me recognize what a wonderful human being I am—this nurtured my ideas, my "univeral I's" and thought reflecting our Navajo ways. They were planted as seeds. I realized that the white American Christian sense was causing me to place my self as second class to

70

everything I do, say and believe. From that time on it became so important to express concerns, objectives, ideas and protest unwanted situations. I was seventeen and ready to soar.

After high school graduation, I attended the Institution of American Indian Arts and Navajo Community College, Tsaile, Arizona.

In Santa Fe I met many other youths—American Indian from all directions of USA. They were unique, doing wondrous work with their talents. I found in myself that the use of language was my best talent. Yet I was last to say what I felt or what I desired to say. I had no woman or real-life experience to write about—but I only imaged. The freshness of my imagination was explosive, daring and exploring—I explored at TAIA. I feel that it is only now that I write with depth to my voice and insights.

As a Navajo woman poet I believe we Navajo women have grown as a nation but should continue to grow. We see ourselves experiencing joyful and tragic events throughout our daily lives. And our thoughts are many ... but they remain unspoken or silently within our minds. I write my wildest thoughts—sometimes they adhere to actual social events but are incoherent to "Navajo ways" of thinking. May many people who read my work gain insights to my ideas, thoughts and understanding of this individual Navajo woman's world. I am now thirty one years old with three beautiful sons.

Morning and Myself

i wake to see the morning
from outside our home
from within me

i walk
to greet dawn boy
    his sister
and their mother i say i am your grandchild
    and that i will
meet you some day

and as that i want to live
 of the flesh of earth
  of the flash of water
  of the flesh of sky

and I will always give
 the soles of my feet
  the water of my mouth
   the sweatbeads of my skin
    the tears of my eyes
     the urine of myself
      the placenta of my babies
and the cleansing water of our hair
              and bodies

to earth
 to water and sky
in peace i go now
in peace we will walk
and in beauty we walk

men tell   and talk

men tell   and talk about their pride
  being so proud of being a father
of so many children born to them
and the joy ride

men do not know   birth and its pain
but i assume those who know the drum tightness
                  do know

they sing reverently
        holding the drum gently
        and the liquid in the drum
        vibrates with good ancient songs

        a woman moans
      the tightness of her drum
       contains unborn life
       and it moves ticklishly touching
      the touching of the baby inside her drum

    at the coming of early morning
     the baby moves
    at the coming of early morning
     hunger teases
    the unborn life

      and the mother laughs

          today many young men deny their birth
          they cast their children upon each other
          and it is they who do not now
          the tightness of the drum, the liquid,
          and the woman's pregnancy

Story Tellers Summer, 1980

Spring thunder
    rumbling
      echoing into Crystal Mountains

i sensed
  the beginning assembly
  of Lightning Ones
  of Thunder Beings
  foot steps pounding in beat
   their beginning blessing dance
  for their summer phase

  Four runners ran
        Children ran
  toward the four directions
       Ordering
    Winter story tellers
      of the earthly-ones
  to halt their humble
      breath of stories
Only on mid-summer day they'll be told
  they ordered
now silence must be
until the Earth has whitened hair

Today
  at the Gallup Welfare Office
  i saw
     two Story tellers
  hushed story tellers
    sat quietly
  nodding their heads
  listening
  to the latest news
  of the acts of Navajos
  and the federal government
  being told on KWYK radio
     in Navajo

The One Who Is Within

Dawn   the sun steadily rose
   angling light
   then casting long shadows
      and the warm loving light

Asdzaa Tsoh Big Woman sat
   feeling   thinking
   and maybe centering
      "the one who stands within"
         unimaginable state of existence
      coolness of morning awaken her
   Naabeeho woman sat
   sipping deep sunset deep sunset orange tea
         making her family fire bread
         i knew her once

Some days i walk   just walk along
      some times i sense an assault of dark rains
and "the one who stands inside" makes an alliance
   with Rain souls
   me—the smell of wet dirt i long for

   Naabeeho woman in the female mountains
   Sipping mutton stew dunging fire bread
      i long   to be   to be you
      the smell of cedar wood and hickory on your clothes

Awéé'

Awéé' nishłį́c

shimá dóó shizhé'é

      bijéí bįį honishłbọgo
      do shaáyoonééh át'éeda

A baby   I am
my mother and my father
         in their hearts   I am existing
                      it is so
         no, they do not forget me so

Diane Glancy

I am Poet-in-the-Schools for the Arts and Humanities Council. I had a short story in the University of Mississippi Review, and have been published in over 70 poetry journals. Nimrod, South and West, Poetry Now, Northwoods Journal, Silver Vain, Little Balkans Review, Calyx, Cedar Rock, Windmill, En Passant, Archer, Manna, Sulphur River, Parnassas, Seven Buffaloes, and Bluegrass Literary Review are a few.

In 1981 I won the poetry contest sponsored by the Tulsa Library and in 1982 received a first place award for my poetry from the National Federation of State Poetry Societies.

The American Indian Theater Company gave me first place in their playwriting contest (1982) and I received honorable mention from the Five Civilized Tribes in their contest.

I have my own small, fine arts press, called Myrtle Wood. I am a graduate of the University of Missouri, and am currently finishing my MA in Creative Studies at Central State University in Edmond.

A chapbook of my Indian poetry is scheduled for publication in 1984 by Blue Cloud Quarterly.

Two Animals, One Flood

Day after day they caught rain in the smoke-hole
        of the teepee, sewed with curved bone
and porcupine quill, the ground limp with
                matted grass,
stalk upon stalk like thin ancestors.
        We cup our hands with their anguished
smoke and frizzled fire. Thickets bend like ancient
                women; barbed-wire
thickets of the white man never will have leaves,
        though they wait all summer.
                        Our tires braid the mud.
refinery-smoke makes old campfires.
                Noah's wife closes the
hole of her one-window ark. Husks of buffalo
        laugh at animals in the stalls. Fires hiss
                in the eyes of children.
Animals stand two by two, but there is only one
                        flood.

There Won't Be Another

The large porcupine breathes smaller ones
        from his mouth. They rise,
curve backward, and arch over the large one.
        They run from blazing grills of
cars and slammed suburban doors.
                Spotted hens, red deer, lope with
them on the prairie, plug-in the rain, hand-weld
                waves to canoe.
Loose strings of light hang from antlers in the
                backyard of outerspace.
Shut out, torn away, the burning Christ still
                rises on the water.
        The porcupine speaks to himself
                from the small rainbow of porcupines.
He paddles the canoe-ark with deer and prairie hens
                over the rabbiteye and red haw.

Mary Ackerman, 1938, Eugene Buechel Photograph Museum of Modern Art, New York

She wears trousers,
stands with her weight on one leg more than on
the other,
self-conscious and serious as a reservation school.
Her dark hair shines like a horse-mane,
the plaid shirt probably her brother's.
The bulky car before which she stands, mud-splattered
from the unpaved roads they had.
Now roads are paved,
and cars
not as stocky as they were, nor always black.
But an Indian girl in trousers is more common, and
photographs still reflect a young girl
before an awkward car.

Looking for My Old Indian Grandmother in the Summer Heat of 1980

The heat uncovers the window and attic-fan
that pulls in more heat.

It was like this in fifty-four, they say,
and I remember, somehow, the hot, white air in the
percale curtains at the window.

It comes back to me now.
I think it was the year my grandmother died.

I look into the trunk, and under the rock
that is her grave.
It was in 1954. July 14.

Her hands and face turn hard before we arrive.
We are bleached clean from her responsibility.

It all happened before I was old enough to ask,
before she knew I would even want to know.

It is because I am more like her than the others
I want to know what rock it is
she left upturned.

Lunar Eclipse

I
Earth's shadow crosses the full-
moon in a dark corridor.
It is the place we made under
Loutre's dining-table
on the reservation.
Legs of heavy chairs, table-
cloth almost to the seats.
We had to get under the table to
dust the legs of chairs.
Our dark images stored
so many craters of the moon:
thistles by the mission road
like flamingos in books,
their necks, curved pipes my
father pulled from under the house
when he rebuilt the kitchen.
Dancing Deer and Deer Rattle called
the Indian agent.
We heard them at Loutre's
under the dining-table.
Houses weren't ours to remake.
Father's eyes grew large as a flamingo's
when Loutre came to our house.
His shadow on the cratered floor
of the kitchen
crossed father's eyes like a
slow blink.
We see it again in the eclipse of the moon
dusting substance more dense than light.

II
Earth's shadow crosses the full moon.
It says a moment, then passes.
They meet like
two old soldiers with the war behind them,
masked in grief it was over so soon.

It is the moon that left the hollow of
the ocean, they say,
but could not flee to the far heavens.
It remains to orbit the earth
only occasionally reminded it is outranked.

Mary Goose

    My favorite form of fantasyland in my early years was reading. When I discovered creating writing at Iowa State University, the fantasyland began to include a blank piece of paper. I know that I have always had an imagination; writing is an outlet for that.

    The only inclination that I would ever want to write was the idea I had ever since I discovered Science Fiction long ago. It was to write Science Fiction. My love of reading for any type of books got started by having my mother translate comic books into Mesquakie for me before I learned to read.

    I'm a full blooded Native American of the Mesquakie and Chippewa tribes, presently living in Des Moines, Iowa. My mother is a member of the Mesquakie tribe and my influences are from that tribe. We lived at the Mesquakie Settlement near Tama, Iowa, until I was in the third grade. I started out at Iowa State University at Ames, Iowa, planning to be a Veterinarian, and ended up with a BA in Anthropology with minors in Art and American Indian Studies.

    This anthology will be the first publication of my poetry. For the time being, I will continue to write poetry and short fiction and work on getting more published. I have found writing to be one place I can be an artist, anthropologist, and one big dreamer.

Insight

Was it the brown Eagle feather that
    fell from the dancers' mostly gold clothing,
    the feather with the white tip that was
    given a special song and tradition allowed
    four traditional men dancers who, by being
    veterans, earned honor of being chosen
    to dance for the feather and pick it up
        just the way it's always been done
Was it the smell of coffee, fry bread, the corn soup
    that came into existence at the outside
    edge of the round wooden arbor
In Bismarck
That made me remember

That one day, years ago

Of the first time I ever saw grandmother cry
    her eyes no longer seeing
    the eye of the needle, the thread only
    a faded reminder of the cataracts
Not having seen the grease get too hot, as it
    was cooking on her low, fire-charred
    iron grill over the open fire

That was only magnifying

The small fire in the black cast iron skillet
    and her fears

Grandfather, the one who said that
    women were the ones to cook, sew, wash,
    told my aunt to take her inside   Then
He finished her cooking,   the simmering corn soup,
    her fully brewed coffee kept warm by the low fire
    at the outer edge of the grill

My mother and aunts nearby
    let him finish   with no visible intervention.

Cornfield Myth

Walking through a field
 between rows of corn stalks
caught in the small hot summer
 air that has been stuck for
so long in the field

Hot Sun that can burn bright
 young red berries ripe/dark
doing spot checks here and there
 to see if the earth is still there
the toes of the corn dug deep
 into the dry starched gray soil

Remains of past inhabitants
 uprooted by extending corn roots
  flake remains chipped off
   long ago forming stone tools
  shards of someones once white china
  a rusting can of Coke

Warm blood turning into torrents
 of red colored water
a so-called gully washer
 my foot cut by a piece of
jagged brown beer bottle glass
 the dirt hungrily drinking up
each individual drop

The corn deceived into thinking
 it is a hot summer rain
yellow corn turning different
 colors, ... pink, red, purple ...

And for a moment I know that
 Indian Corn used to be yellow
Long, long ago one hot summer day.

Last Night in Sisseton, S. D.

There was heat lightning out west
The clown of the pow-wow circuit
    reminded me of a swamp marigold,
    daring to sit in his multi-colored lawn chair
    right in the middle of the puddle
       of last night's rain
Wind muffled voices moving around
An old green army tent was flapping in the wind,
    sounding just like the wind hitting
    plastic over a window in winter.

All night long, headlights leading other headlights
    from
    dusty dirt road to
    dark concrete with
    a white line   to
    noise, ten o'clock news,
    steamy cement.

How quiet is the Sun, when it is rising?
How quiet is the dust as it settles?
I couldn't tell you.

Ask me again, after next fourth of July.

Rain! Then I would have a reason to get in
    the car and leave.

Then ...
    Some winter night I can sit,
    listen to my tapes of songs,
    and look at photographs
    of summer pow-wows   with
    sounds of tents flapping
    in the background.

Just an Old Man

With
Tattered gray fishnet eyes,
Body respiration submersible,
Eyes that catch clear ripples,
    just like us,
Eyes that touch sandy bottoms,
    unlike us,
Dialogues to the past,
And present acquaintances,
Like me, his grandchild,
A Cultural detective.
And I
Who seeks beneath and under,
The skin of the water,
The footprints deep inside,
Where the red water breaths,
Memories to fish that sparkle,
In the daylight within,
The clear visible ripples,
And unseen sandy bottoms.
From both I learn.

Friends

You know there were others before you,
But most saw me as a failure in their terms:
Saying the driftwood I kept was only
A dried-up piece of wood, not the Hawks'
Wing I saw in the shape   and claiming the
Nautilus on the shelf was only absorbing
Dust into its spiral.

Those "friends" were around long enough for
Me to start mourning for myself in the
Funereal silence,   of the quiet collapse
Of the inner chambers of the Nautilus;
The shriveling of the wrinkles in the
Wood   So much that my lungs
Began to deflate from the painless
Event of watching and began to seep
Down into my socks and shoes.

But I don't have to tell you all this.
I know what you mean when you say
The inside of you is like Earth
Bomb-pitted with Contentment and the
Pain of Breathing.

Photo by Jeanne Kobos Lupien

Janet Campbell Hale

Born Jan. 11, 1946 in L.A. Raised in the Coeur d'Alene reservation in northern Idaho and the Yakima reservation in Washington. I am primarily a novelist but I am a poet too—albeit a minor poet. B.A. UC Berkeley 1974, M.A. UC Davis 1983. Attended law school for two years. Mother of a grown son and an eleven year old daughter. I am finishing the last draft of my new novel. It has been hard work. I'll be glad to be finished, glad to shake the Davis dust from my feet and get on down the road.

Backyard Swing

Did you ever
Swing in my swing
Behind our house
In Worley?
The house is still there
But the tree is gone.
My father made me
That swing,
You must remember—
The heavy rope
Tied around the
Sturdy branch,
Two of us could
Swing together.

Did you ever,
While way up high,
Close your eyes and drop
Your head way back,
Open eyes,
glimpse patches of sky
Through leafy branches,
Look at
Leaves, shimmering
green on one side,
Dull grey on the other,
Leaves shimmering
When the wind
Moved them?

You must remember
That tree and that swing.
The house is still there,
Windowless and stepless,
Without insides,
Groaning when the
Wind moves it.

Walls of Ice

Like the sun frozen
Still in the faded sky,
Like the surface of the
River
In the dead of winter
She slowed,
And slowed,
And finally stopped,
Her body bent
And twisted:
Stopped,
Almost,
Except for her
Clouded green eyes
Always moving,
Following,
Looking
Though her vision
perceives only vague images;
And, except for her
Voice, strained, as
raspy as it is,
(The voice that used to
Sing, sing, so fully,
So rich and pure)
Her voice continues on,
Her words repeat themselves,
Come round again,
Over and over
Fall heavily upon me
When she says she dreams of him,
Every night
It's just like he's come back.
No, it's like she's going away!
I want to hang onto her
I want to keep her
from fading into that
World she always talks about
That exists only in
Her memories,
Hang onto her stiffened, gnarled hands,
Before she drifts away
Again,
Dissolves into the blue
Walls of her room,
The room she never leaves,
Damned blue walls
Like water all around
Enclosing her,
Like walls of ice
Freezing her,
Making her unable to move

Her voice
  puts forth words
  Faintly as if
From far away
Like the echo
of footsteps
Her words
Tell of last night's
dream and all those
memories of seventy-eight
years
  Memories scrambled and
randomly chosen,
And the words become
Slower,
And slower
Each time.

Scene From a Dream

Frozen, rotting, dark leaves
Cover the path through the woods.
The light is dim:
Late afternoon of
An overcast day.

My little daughter
Walks with me and inside
My body is a baby
Although it isn't apparent,
And I don't feel it move,
Still I feel its presence,
A secret, private presence,
Safe, hidden,
Carried effortlessly.

The day is very dark and cold.
I have been drinking with
People I don't know
In a noisy and crowded place.
I was a young girl
While I was there,
While I was drinking,
Laughing and dancing
With strange men.

On this path I am me again:
Growing older, older,
All the time.
I hold my daughter's hand
For comfort.

Desmet, Idaho, March 1969

At my father's wake,
The old people
      Knew me,
   Though I
      Knew them not,
And spoke to me
In our tribe's
Ancient tongue,
Ignoring
The fact
That I
Don't speak
The language.
And so
I listened
As if I understood
What it was all about,
And,
Oh,
How it
Stirred me
To hear again
That strange,
    Softly
    Flowing
Native tongue,
So
Familiar to
My childhood ear.

Custer Lives in Humboldt County

What was it called,
When all that old-time white man trouble
was going on?
All that killing and taking away of home,
of country?
Justifiable genocide or some
such thing, no doubt.
Involuntary manslaughter,
they called it,
When that cop in Humboldt county
Shot the young Pomo last spring,
Shot him and left him
Lying by the roadside,
Hidden in the tall green grass,
Lying bleeding in the spring sunlight,
In the tall green grass,
Involuntary manslaughter,
they called it,
when the Pomo died at last.

All the old, wild-West white man trouble
is over now,
Should be forgotten, they say.
Wild grass grows again at Little Big Horn,
at Steptoe, at Wounded Knee,
Tall grass, swaying in the gentle wind,
covering the old battle scars,
The old healed wounds.
The sun shines warm in a big, clear sky,
All is quiet now,
The past is best forgotten.

Fall 1973
Berkeley, California

Where Have All The Indians Gone?

"Lookatitthisway: I have seen some
Blue-eyed blondes Who're more Indian
than some full-bloods", Ego-tripping
bunch of goddamned Indians deciding
who is Indian and who is not and then
there was that blonde guy from Germany
who hung around D-Q and said there was
no such thing as a full-blood anyway
and maybe there isn't and I
Personally know white people who pre-
tend to be Indian (grownups, mind you)
who go around talking about how they are
discriminated against on account of race,
retelling an incident in which some white
person took one look at them and began mis-
treating them because of their Indianness
(But any fool can see that they are white
and nobody can imagine anyone mistaking
them for anything else but you've got to
listen to their "discriminated against" story
because you're polite and anyway you like
them and don't want to hurt their feelings)
And some even take on an "Indian name" and
write "Indian poetry" full of allusion to
and images of Eagle Feathers and Swift
Deer and Mother Earth and maybe a little
Corn Pollen for good measure and reference
to The Four Directions that's all you really
need to do in order to sound real Indianny
don't you know and they run around with this
"More Indian than thou" attitude
Because they didn't belong in their own white
Culture and need to therefore have a reason
Why they did not claiming one drop of Indian
blood or maybe even no Indian blood just an
"Indian heart, Indian soul" Therefore having
a reason for being an outsider and what the hell
Being Indian is as good an excuse as anyone
Could wish for and yet we know, really, don't
we, all of us deep down, even the pretenders
That we are Indian who didn't even necessarily
want to be but just are and everyone always knew
it and everyone could see it and our parents were
Indian and we lived on reservations and have brown
skin and black hair and have truly known discrimination
on account of race and then there are these people
running around saying some blue-eyed blondes are
more Indian than we are it makes my stomach want
to turn.

March, 1984
Davis, California

Joy Harjo

Joy Harjo was born in Tulsa, Oklahoma in 1951, and is of the Creek Tribe. She is the author of The Last Song, *and* What Moon Drove Me To This, *both collections of poetry. Currently she lives in Sante Fe and is working on a screenplay and a new poetry collection.*

I am from Oklahoma. But that isn't my only name.
I am Creek and other Oklahoma/Arkansas people. I am
a woman, many women. The namings can go on and on and
it is frustrating to name someone or something when in
the real *world all is in motion, in a state of change.*
That's why there is a danger when you try to name with
one name what is many, has no sides and is round. But
there has to be a focal point or all would be diffused.
And I am here, alive and now, and speaking.

We are all creators. We breathe. To speak is to form
breath and to make manifest sound into the world. As
I write I create myself again and again. Re-Create. And
breathe. And I see that I am not one voice, but many:

all colors, all sounds, all fears, all loves... But
they focus into one, to have meaning in a world that is
really one dimensional in terms of all the thousands of
dimensions that there are. We have learned to only touch
so much. That is why I write. I want to touch more, to
know the inner caverns of myself that are light years away
but as close as the air   breathing in   breathing out.

I love language, sound, how emotions, images, dreams
are formed in air and on the page. When I was a little
kid in Oklahoma I would get up before everyone else and
go outside to a place of dark rich earth next to the
foundation of the house. I would dig piles of earth
with a stick, smell it, form it. It had sound. Maybe
that's when I first learned to write poetry, even though
I never really wrote until I was in my early twenties.

We learn to identify the world by the language that we
speak. At this point in my life I know only English
well, not enough Creek (Muskogee), and some Navajo.
As I grow older, write more, sense more, I have come to
feel that English is not enough. It is a male language,
not tribal, not spiritual enough. It is hard to speak

certain concepts, certain visions, certain times and
places in the English language. Again, maybe that's
why I write poetry, because poetry can work with the
language, manipulate it so that it can embrace those
concepts, visions, times and places that the language
in and of itself can't do.

I feel strongly that I have a responsibility to all
the sources that I am: to all past and future ancestors,
to my home country, to all places that I touch down
on and that are myself, to all voices, all women, all
of my tribe, all people, all earth and beyond that to
all beginnings and endings. In a strange kind of sense
it frees me to believe in myself, to be able to speak,
to have voice, because I have to; it is my survival.

April 1981

Anchorage

for Audre Lorde

This city is made of stone, of blood, and fish.
There are Chugatch Mountains to the east
and whale and seal to the west.
It hasn't always been this way, because glaciers
who are ice ghosts create oceans, carve earth
and shape this city here, by the sound.
They swim backwards in time.

Once a storm of boiling earth cracked open
the streets, threw open the town.
It's quiet now, but underneath the concrete
is the cooking earth,
      and above that, air
which is another ocean, where spirits we can't see
are dancing   joking   getting full
on roasted caribou, and the praying
goes on, extends out.

Nora and I go walking down 4th Avenue
and know it is all happening.
On a park bench we see someone's Athabascan
grandmother, folded up, smelling like 200 years
of blood and piss, her eyes closed against some
unimagined darkness, where she is buried in an ache
in which nothing makes
      sense.

We keep on breathing, walking, but softer now,
the clouds whirling in the air above us.
What can we say that would make us understand
better than we do already?
Except to speak of her home and claim her
as our own history, and know that our dreams
don't end here, two blocks away from the ocean
where our hearts still batter away at the muddy shore.

And I think of the 6th Avenue jail, of mostly Native
and Black men, where Henry told about being shot at
eight times outside a liquor store in L.A., but when
the car sped away he was surprised he was alive,
no bullet holes, man, and eight cartridges strewn
on the sidewalk
     all around him.

Everyone laughed at the impossibility of it,
but also the truth. Because who would believe
the fantastic and terrible story of all of our survival
those who were never meant
      to survive?

Remember

Remember the sky that you were born under,
know each of the star's stories.
Remember the moon, know who she is. I met her
in a bar once in Iowa City.
Remember the sun's birth at dawn, that is the
strongest point of time. Remember sundown
and the giving away to night.
Remember your birth, how your mother struggled
to give you form and breath. You are evidence of
her life, and her mother's, and hers.
Remember your father. He is your life, also.
Remember the earth whose skin you are:
red earth, black earth, yellow earth, white earth
brown earth, we are earth.
Remember the plants, trees, animal life who all have their
tribes, their families, their histories, too. Talk to them,
listen to them. They are alive poems.
Remember the wind. Remember her voice. She knows the
origin of this universe. I heard her singing Kiowa war
dance songs at the corner of Fourth and Central once.
Remember that you are all people and that all people
are you.
Remember that you are this universe and that this
universe is you.
Remember that all is in motion, is growing, is you.
Remember that language comes from this.
Remember the dance that language is, that life is.
Remember.

New Orleans

This is the south. I look for evidence
of other Creeks, for remnants of voices,
or for tobacco brown bones to come wandering
down Conti Street, Royale, or Decatur.
Near the French Market I see a blue horse
caught frozen in stone in the middle of
a square. Brought in by the Spanish on
an endless ocean voyage he became mad
and crazy. They caught him in blue
rock, said
        don't talk.

I know it wasn't just a horse
           that went crazy.

Nearby is a shop with ivory and knives.
There are red rocks. The man behind the
counter has no idea that he is inside
magic stones. He should find out before
they destroy him. These things
have memory,
           you know.

I have a memory.
          It swims deep in blood,
a delta in the skin. It swims out of Oklahoma,
deep the Mississippi River. It carries my
feet to these places: the French Quarter,
stale rooms, the sun behind thick and moist
clouds, and I hear boats hauling themselves up
and down the river.

My spirit comes here to drink.
My spirit comes here to drink.
Blood is the undercurrent.

There are voices buried in the Mississippi
mud. There are ancestors and future children
buried beneath the currents stirred up by
pleasure boats going up and down.
There are stories here made of memory.

I remember DeSoto. He is buried somewhere in
this river, his bones sunk like the golden
treasure he traveled half the earth to find,
came looking for gold cities, for shining streets
of beaten gold to dance on with silk ladies.

He should have stayed home.

              (Creeks knew of him for miles
               before he came into town.
                Dreamed of silver blades
                and crosses.)

And knew he was one of the ones who yearned
for something his heart wasn't big enough
to handle.
                    (And DeSoto thought it was gold.)

The Creeks lived in earth towns,
                          not gold,
             spun children, not gold.
That's not what DeSoto thought he wanted to see.
The Creeks knew it, and drowned him in
             the Mississippi River
                    so he wouldn't have to drown himself.

Maybe his body is what I am looking for
as evidence. To know in another way
that my memory is alive.
But he must have got away, somehow,
because I have seen New Orleans,
the lace and silk buildings,
trolley cars on beaten silver paths,
graves that rise up out of soft earth in the rain,
shops that sell black mammy dolls
holding white babies.

And I know I have seen DeSoto,
                    having a drink on Bourbon Street,
                    mad and crazy
                    dancing with a woman as gold
                    as the river bottom.

She Had Some Horses

She had some horses.

She had horses who were bodies of sand.
She had horses who were maps drawn of blood.
She had horses who were skins of ocean water.
She had horses who were the blue air of sky.
She had horses who were fur and teeth.
She had horses who were clay and would break.
She had horses who were splintered red cliff.

She had some horses.

She had horses with long, pointed breasts.
She had horses with full, brown thighs.
She had horses who laughed too much.
She had horses who threw rocks at glass houses.
She had horses who licked razor blades.

She had some horses.

She had horses who danced in their mothers' arms.
She had horses who thought they were the sun and their
bodies shone and burned like stars.
She had horses who waltzed nightly on the moon.
She had horses who were much too shy, and kept quiet
in stalls of their own making.

She had some horses.

She had horses who liked Creek Stomp Dance songs.
She had horses who cried in their beer.
She had horses who spit at male queens who made
them afraid of themselves.
She had horses who said they weren't afraid.
She had horses who lied.
She had horses who told the truth, who were stripped
bare of their tongues.

She had some horses.

She had horses who called themselves, "horse".
She had horses who called themselves, "spirit", and kept
their voices secret and to themselves.
She had horses who had no names.
She had horses who had books of names.

She had some horses.

She had horses who whispered in the dark, who were afraid to speak.
She had horses who screamed out of fear of the silence, who
carried knives to protect themselves from ghosts.
She had horses who waited for destruction.
She had horses who waited for resurrection.

She had some horses.

She had horses who got down on their knees for any saviour.
She had horses who thought their high price had saved them.
She had horses who tried to save her, who climbed in her
bed at night and prayed as they raped her.

She had some horses.

She had some horses she loved.
She had some horses she hated.

These were the same horses.

Crossing The Border Into Canada

We looked the part.
It was past midnight, well into
the weekend. Coming out of Detroit
into the Canada side. Border guards
and checks. We are asked, "Who are you Indians,
and which side are you from?"
Barney answers in a broken English.
He talks this way to white people
not to us. "Our kids."
My children are wrapped
and sleeping in the backseat.
He points with his lips to half-eyed
Richard in the front. "That one, too."
But Richard looks like he belongs
to no one. Just sits there wild-haired
like a Menominee would. "And my wife."
Not true. But hidden under the windshield
at the edge of this country we feel immediately
suspicious. These questions, and we don't look
like we belong to either side.

"Any liquor or firearms?" He should
have asked that years ago. And we can't help
but laugh. Kids stir around in the backseat, but
it is the border guard who is anxious.
He is looking for crimes, stray horses
for which he has no apparent evidence.

"Where are you going?" Indians
in an Indian car trying to find a
Delaware powwow that was barely mentioned
in Milwaukee. Northern singing and
the northern sky. Moon in a colder air.
Not sure of the place, but knowing the name
we ask, "Moravian Town?"

The border guard thinks he might have
the evidence. It pleases him. Past midnight.
Stars out clear into Canada and he knows only to ask,
"Is it a bar?"

Crossing the border into Canada, we are
silent. Lights and businesses we drive toward
could be America, too. Following us
into the north.

Gordon Henry

I am of Ojibwa and French ancestry and was born in Philadelphia, Pennsylvania in 1955.

Both of my parents were raised at Pine Point on the White Earth Reservation in Minnesota.

In 1954 my father joined the Navy and, as a result, my family lived in many places across the U.S. and its territories; with some of the time in between Naval Stations spent on the reservation.

At the present time, I live in East Lansing, Michigan with my wife Mary Anne and my 1 year old daughter, Kehli. I am a student at Michigan State University where I am working on my Masters degree in Creative Writing.

Basically, my poetry almost always stems from vision and the significance of the moment as suspended in vision's written work.

I realize that's very general and could apply to a great deal of poetry, but I am, in many respects, looking for what a vision or an image can imply in the form of words. Each vision's remembrance has a life of its own.

Outside White Earth

Vision and breath
travel away in
the smell of rain.
Next to a pickup
an old man stands
sleeping drunk,
hand on zipper.
        Leave him.
There is the liquor store.
Jukebox shadows of music
coming back around again
and again.
Torrents of faces,
chased glasses
and wives.
Shapes of smoke
opening mouths opening
restroom doors almost
as frequently.

At the touch of a hand
leaving, rain fills
your ears from the
roof, crumbling you
awake. You
stand,
        hand on zipper,
face against a phone
number
on the paint
of a peeling wall.

Pine Point, you are:

            black ash
            photographs of
            Korean-crazed uncles,
            burnt in
            corner rooms of
            old shacks.

you are morning gray mist
            covering the fields
            and the four steps to the
            front door of the church.

you are   nicks in the doorway
of the guild hall
where undertakers
and uncles couldn't
get the casket through
very easily.

you are   wind smacking
screen doors up against
places with windows,
boarded and empty.

you are   windshield cracked
afternoons laying
shadows on spring busted
upholstery of cars turned
over in yards.

you are   smoking hair
of gasolined cats
burning in wide
schoolyard eyes.

you are   sinking in a
ditch like a beer
can sunk at an
angle like headstones
across the road.

you are   underneath
leaves an old man
burns in the bottom
of a barrel at dusk.

you are   wake
songs like smoke
whispers from stovepipe
chimneys, separating
between branches
of trees to nothing
between stars.

you are   reservation migrant
drunk eyes open
against cold linoleum,
gone to a television
test pattern

in the city.

Freeze Tag

Evening comes
between astral
radiance, pulsing
in the blood
and a distance
of voices.

In the game
you became
frozen, chased
far away
from the summer
front yard
and your recently
unwrapped birthday
presents on
a picnic table.

You were chased
and tagged
after tripping
over a log
as you were
looking over
your shoulder.

In the game
you are frozen,
forgotten,
too far away
to be touched
free from the evening
a distance
of dying
voices.

You are frozen
in the
game
in air cooling
leaves falling
and in a
distance of
dying voices.

You wonder
who is
it
now.

Waking On A Greyhound

From far away
Rice Lake loons
call
the distance
darkening,
in whatever was
dream, fading
as crows
lift, piece
by piece,
from dead
on the side
of the road.

Leaving Smoke's

To Smoke and Claudia

Black
wings sun glanced
green, crows
circle and half circle
snowfields before scattering
over old barns falling
slowly paintless
against the sky

across the road.

Your car shivers
to start, windshield
trembling, Sky Blue
barked breath floating
white through
fences behind his
back and the door
opening she waves from.

At the stop sign,

the prism hanging
between the door curtains
still turns
sun colors
on the kitchen
floor.

On M-66

something or the wind
moves outside
and turns his head to
windowed dusk's sun
leaving behind barns
with glazed empty
snowfields
beyond the prism
still.

Lance Henson

Lance Henson, Cheyenne, poet, raised near Calumet, Oklahoma. An ex-marine, member Black Belt Karate Association, member Cheyenne Dog Soldier Warrior Society, also a member of the Native American Church. Poetry has been published in every major anthology of Native American Poetry including:
THE REMEMBERED EARTH—Red Earth Press, Albuquerque, N.M.
CARRIERS OF THE DREAM WHEEL—Harper & Row
VOICES OF THE RAINBOW—Viking Press
AMERICAN INDIAN LITERATURE—O. U. Press
THE FIRST SKIN AROUND ME—Sinte Gleska, South Dakota

Henson has published six books of poetry:
KEEPER OF ARROWS—Renaissance Press, Johnstown, Penn.
NAMING THE DARK—Point Riders Press, Norman, Okla.
MISTA—Strawberry Press, New York, N.Y.
BUFFALO MARROW ON BLACK—Full Count Press, Edmond, Okla.
IN A DARK MIST—Cultural Communications Press, Long Island
ANOTHER DISTANCE—Full Count Press, Edmond, Okla.

Books forthcoming:
A CIRCLING REMEMBRANCE—Spotted Hawk Press, Tulsa, Okla.
DARK FIR—Genemuiden, Netherlands

A dozen copies of NAMING THE DARK were smuggled to dissident writers in the Soviet Union by a Russian Poet. Henson's works are presently being translated into Dutch, Sicilian and Macedonian.

poem near midway truck stop

along the turner turnpike at a rest stop between
oklahoma city and tulsa
i feel the morning sun inch over the leaves of a small elm
rising to the scent of sage and wildflowers i lean on one
elbow

beyond the field the sound of cars and a lone water tower
mark a small town
i remove the knife from under the sleeping bag
and place it in the sheath on my hip.

*ho hatama hestoz na no me
it is july
i imagine coffee in a pale cup on a wooden table
far from here
and look west toward home

*there is a powerful trembling around me
                                      (Cheyenne)

vision song (cheyenne)

the scent of sage
          and sweetgrass braids

a man
saying goodbye

to himself

north

north of my grandfathers house
shadows of first winter storm walk
the fields toward the south canadian

without a word
the pregnant dog i have tried
to be rid of for weeks
has gone

in the house my daughter
has disappeared into
dream

her small trembling hands
flower into a cold wind that smells
of the moon

at chadwicks bar and grill

a sky the color of a wrens breath
hangs over red clouds
hint of rain
and home is dirt underfoot
tu fu and li po have
forgiven nothing
not waking drunk under any moon
or the incessant calling
of a loon
so waiting is the roses own
signature
the spider catches the fly
at morning
whether i am there
or not

buffalo marrow on black

wind of sage in which the world dreams
        strike the earth where i have walked
                          let my relatives hear this
scent of cedar pass tonight over the faces of the sleeping
        world and the paths of the sick and troubled and weak
brother sun
        help me to be remembered among all growing things
sister water
        grandfather fire

                        muts i mi u na

                            wo is ta

                    henah haneh
                        henah haneh

buffalo calf road woman
        buffalo woman
                this is all

                this is all

Geary Hobson

I write poems at times when I can't write fiction or nonfiction; at times when because of other work I can't simply find the time to write prose, these poems somehow get written. I wrote most of my poems in the period 1976-1978 when I was an administrator (Director of Native American Studies at University of New Mexico) and when I had to go to all those incredibly boring meetings with other department heads or other university administrators. Most of the junk said at those meetings was the tired old rehashed gobbledegook that I had heard at other meetings, so I found a way of sitting back in my chair away from the table and scribbling at my notebook. While everybody else thought I was probably taking notes on the "Important Meeting," I was actually working on poems. It got to where I actually looked forward to those meetings.

Going to the Water

This morning I come to the water again.
It has been a long time.
It has been too long.
    Having the need to pray
I come to the water's edge
where dawn light spreads out
                  over the riverbank
like a blessing of hands.
              the water is cold.
sunlight on the river's surface
diffuses into peacefulness
and adds luster
to the currents of my soul.
    An undertow of grief
lost in fragments of dreams
              broken on rocks
carries me calmly
        into the eddy.
    I face the east
and breathe gently to the sun.
I am praying softly:
    I turn northward
and talk to the wind.
    I turn westward,
and last to south.
          I bathe my body,
touching my face
         and the coolness of water
prays with me.
    I am reluctant to leave the cold stream
but my prayer
at least this part of it
is nearly finished
         and I go shoreward
to burn red tobacco
for the earth's new morning
for the river's new earth.

Lonnie Kramer

The morning is hot and windy.
What more to expect of March
in its last days
than wind and dust?

but this morning I meet
an old ghost from the '60's:
Lonnie Kramer
(bony elbows skimpy moustache
pimpled face) now as then
Though then executive chairman
of the campus Young Socialist Alliance
who once condemned me
as a capitalist lackey
stating to the assembled true-believers
in an evening meeting
how I craved beer bourbon shots
and pool games in a railroaders' bar
a scuzzy place patronized by
Pimas Papagos bikers
hippies and needle-freaks
He impaled me with the charge
I didn't think constantly
of Marx Lenin Che
and the workers of the world
or what national HQ
thought we should do
(when to march when to strike
when to shit and what color)
and I guess he was right.

And now Lonnie
chief regional salesman
of Dutton (or Bratton?) Industries
makers of microwave ovens
and other assorted time-saving gadgets
for the American homemaker
with a territory
"big as all outdoors"
with "the sky as limit."

We talk over old times
though not about national HQ
or Marx and Che
The March wind carries our words
like feathers

toward the city's outskirts
half-heard   and half-listened to
lost in dust and heat.
The frayed elbows of my jacket
are under his close scrutiny
and I see he doesn't approve
my long hair either.

I still know very little
about microwave ovens
even less about Dutton (or Bratton?)
Industries.
But I still like beer   bourbon shots
pool   games
I still hang out in scuzzy bars
full of Indians   street-people
and other workers of the world.

For My Brother and Sister
Southwestern Indian Poets

I come from a wet land
    (bayous   hills   old stomp-dance
     grounds   flood-plain delta)
and I never learned to sing for rain.

Barbara's Land Revisited—August 1978

This time you're with me
and we pull into Claude
much cooler than it was that other time
thanks to your new Toyota's air-conditioning.

The clouds around the town
are still buffalo-shaped
and dust-devils still skitter
along the interstate.
Claude's like a white adhesive bandage
lying on the blister
of the Staked Plains' northern rump
and we come to the same ice-cream stand
though now called the Dairy Mart.

Claude looks like it's changed a bit.
"Prog-gressed"—as they say here.
A big new grain elevator loomed
a bland castle of commerce
as we came into town from the west.
I see they've got a new Chevy place
spic-'n'-span models all ready to roll.
Yes   things have changed.

Meanwhile   back at the Dairy Mart
(formerly the Tastee Freeze)
Connie Sue—as her name tag says—
waits to take our orders.
"What y'all gonna have?"
And as usual you take all day
to make up your mind.
but I know what I want.
"I'll have a chocolate milkshake"
Connie Sue smiles   she is young
blond high-school seniorish
probably dreaming of fall cheerleader tryouts.

I drink the milkshake
celebrating this time nothing in particular
no Comanche centennial no Palo Duro Canyon fight.
with you here with me   there's at least
one Comanche now in Claude again.

I'm feeling good about Claude
as we leave heading east—Oklahoma-bound.
The browning-green land all around
Connie Sue who was "nice as pie"
as they say here.
Feeling good that is until someways
out of Claude   and a state cop pulls us over.
"Lemme see your driver's li-cense"
and all the old fear comes back
the wound beneath the flesh.

Claude, I'm not writing anymore poems about you.

Tiger People

(for Joy Harjo)

1.

Lying along the wide branch
in a fist of gathered tension,
the panther waits, watching her prey.
    When the panther springs,
you will see such a motion
of fluid grace—like blinding lightning
framed in frozen rock.
    The cubs watch their mother,
eyes wide with love and awe—
by her example they will learn
grace and beauty
and how to survive in a hostile world.

2.

I make it down to the stomp-dance grounds
                            early.
In the back of a beat-up pickup,
two men and a woman quietly sing
Muscogee songs, and check the turtle-shell
                            rattles
before the dancing begins.
    There is such calm-enshrouded tension,
betrayed only by the motion of expectant eyes.

It is going to be a good dance.

Linda Hogan

Born in 1947, tribal affiliation Chickasaw. M.A. in English and Creative Writing from the University of Colorado. I have taught American Indian Literature at CU and Colorado College, creative writing at Colorado Women's College, CU. I've worked as Poet-in-Residence with Oklahoma and Colorado Arts Councils since 1980, and have given workshops and lectures in a variety of places. My experience as a reader has taken me to ten states, several universities and colleges, Indian communities, and conferences.

Three books of poems: Calling Myself Home, *(Greenfield Review Press),* Daughters, I Love You *(Loretto Heights Monograph Series), and* Eclipse *(UCLA American Indian Center Press, due out later this year). I have just completed a first novel,* The Grace of Wooden Birds, *and have one unpublished poetry mss.* The Diary of Amanda McFadden.

I have published hundreds of poems and short stories in nearly fifty magazines, among them The Little Magazine, Prairie Schooner, Beloit Poetry Journal, Painted Bride Quarterly, Ark's Rexroth Issue, Denver Quarterly, Beyond Baroque, Greenfield Review, Conditions, Blue Buildings. *I have had poems and stories anthologized in fifteen books:* The Remembered Earth *(Red Earth Press),* Southwest Fiction Anthology, Gnosis Anthology of Contemporary American and Russian Literature and Art *(Columbia University, NY.),* Ariadne's Thread *(Harper & Row),* Reweaving the Web of Life *(New Society Publishers), an American Indian anthology in Macedonian and one in Sicilian, the* International Women's Peace Anthology, *and others.*

Song for My Name

Before sunrise
think of brushing out an old woman's
dark braids.
Think of your hands,
fingertips on the soft hair.

If you have this name,
your grandfather's dark hands
lead horses toward the wagon
and a cloud of dust follows,
ghost of silence.

That name is full of women
with black hair
and men with eyes like night.
It means no money
tomorrow.

Such a name my mother loves
while she works gently
in the small house.
She is a white dove
and in her own land
the mornings are pale,
birds sing into the white curtains
and show off their soft breasts.

If you have a name like this,
there's never enough water.
There is too much heat.
When lightning strikes, rain
refuses to follow.
It's my name,
that of a woman living
between the white moon
and the red sun, waiting to leave.
It's the name that goes with me
back to earth
no one else can touch.

Blessing

Blessed
are the injured animals
for they live in his cages.
but who will heal my father,
tape his old legs for him?

Here's his bird with the two broken wings
and her feathers are white as an angel
and she says goddamn stirring grains
in the kitchen. When the birds fly out
he leaves the cages open
and she kisses his brow for such
good works.

> Work he says
> all your damned life
> and at the end
> you don't own even a piece of land.

Blessed are the rich
for they eat meat every night.
They have already inherited the earth.

For the rest of us, may we just live
long enough
and unwrinkle our brows,
may we keep our good looks
and some of our teeth
and our bowels regular.

Perhaps we can go live in places
a rich man can't inhabit,
in the sunfish and jackrabbits,
in the cinnamon colored soil,
the land of red grass
and red people
in the valley
of the shadow of Elk
who aren't there.

> He says the old earth
> wobbles so hard, you'd best hang on
> to everything. Your neighbors
> steal what little you got.

Blessed are the rich
for they don't have the same old
Everyday to put up with
like my father
who's gotten old,
> Chickasaw
> chikkih asachi, which means
they left as a tribe not a very great while ago.
They are always leaving, those people.

Blessed
are those who listen
when no one is left to speak.

Cities Behind Glass

Dusty light falls through windows
where entire families journey together, alone.
Mothers open the sills and shake the old world
from lace tablecloths.

Beneath flowered babushkas
immigrant women put their faith in city buses.
They take refuge behind glass,
lay their heads against windows.
Behind veined eyelids
they journey.

Brussels, perhaps, is their destination.
Where older women make lace,
wrapping linen around pins
and where the sun lies down in spider webs.

On the street
invisible panes of glass are strapped
to the sides of a truck.
The world shows through
filled with people, with red horses
making their departures between streets.
Inside that slow horse flesh
behind blinders
the dark animals are running
shadow horses,
horses of light
running across American hills.

Everything is foreign here.
No one sees me.
No one sees this woman walking city streets.
No one sees the animals running inside my skin,
the deep forest of southern trees,
the dark grandmothers looking through my eyes,
taking it in, traveling still.

Saint Coyote

St. Coyote passes over the highway.
His shadow lies down
in headlights,
yellow eyes.
His fur breathing
in busy suburbs where children kneel
with lights dark as shut eyes.

Another world crosses the streets.
Houses vanish.
Square windows are dark
secrets in the ruins.
Shutters wear out
beating on walls.

Luminous savior
wise to traps,
eyes shining like the electric bones
of street lamps,
I heard him last night.
He threw a rock in water
and people followed.
I heard him
beneath a tree, singing
to the disappearing moon
that walks on water.
He was telling it lies about people.

That saint,
always gambling,
crossing dark streets,
walking among skin and shadow,
always lying
about who created death and light.

Black Hills Survival Gathering, 1980

Bodies on fire
the monks in orange cloth
sing morning into light.

Men wake on the hill.
Dry grass blows from their hair.
B52's blow over their heads
leaving a cross on the ground.
Air returns to itself and silence.

Rainclouds are disappearing
with fractures of light in the distance.
Fierce gases forming,
the sky bending
where people arrive
on dusty roads that change
matter to energy.

My husband wakes.
My daughter wakes.
Quiet morning, she stands
in a pail of water
naked, reflecting light
and this man I love,
with kind hands
he washes her slim hips,
narrow shoulders, splashes
the skin containing
wind and fragile fire,
the pulse in her wrist.

My other daughter wakes
to comb warm sun across her hair.
While I make coffee I tell her
this is the land of her ancestors,
blood and heart.
Does her hair become a mane
blowing in the electric breeze,
her eyes dilate and darken?

The sun rises on all of them
in the center of light
hills that have no boundary,
the child named Thunder Horse,
the child named Dawn Protector
and the man
whose name would mean home in Navajo.

At ground zero
in the center of light we stand.
Bombs are buried beneath us,
destruction flies overhead.
We are waking
in the expanding light
the sulphur-colored grass.
A red horse standing on a distant ridge
looks like one burned
over Hiroshima,
silent, head hanging in sickness.
But look
she raises her head
and surges toward the bluing sky.

Radiant morning.
The dark tunnels inside us carry life.
Red.
Blue.
The children's dark hair against my breast.
On the burning hills
in flaring orange cloth
men are singing and drumming
Heartbeat.

Karoniaktatie

"My name is Karoniaktatie, meaning 'Where The Sky Meets The Earth.' It is a good name but not a Turtle Clan name, of which I am a member . . . in other words: I am a turtle . . . slow . . . intermittently thick and thin shelled. Patient, supposedly, but definitely a run of snapping turtle in me."

From 1972-1974 AKWESASNE NOTES poetry editor. Have published my poetry off & on 1974-1982, included in last Akwesasne Notes calendar 1982. In 1972 AKWESASNE NOTES published Native Colours, *first collection of poetry, 88 pages of poetry & illustrations. Head editor of NEWBORN, magazine of Student Publishing Workshop, Institute of American Indian Arts 1977, Santa Fe, New Mexico. Anthologized in* COME TO POWER, 1974, THE NEXT WORLD, 1978, THE REMEMBERED EARTH, 1979.

Elegy

for Lavina,
 Denise,
  Eddie
   & Maxwell

when the old ones die
history is gone/lost/made
all that they know
has been taught
to the younger ones
some has been lost, but
they have guided many
with their words & deeds
& now they are placed
in Creator's hands
to know again their ancestors
we mourn their passing
for we have lost much
we rejoice their passing
for now they have gone
to the Other World
the better place

when the young ones die
it is that many less
who can learn
sacred ways
they could have been
great learners, teachers
we will never know
they were young
women of nations
mothers of clans
to raise up chiefs &
decide the course of nations
but all this is gone
all this we will never know
"the bloom has withered away"
all that is sacred
gone
but let nothing
hinder you
now, on your path
to the Creation.

a farmer
a big man
a good & kind man
so much to teach
we had so much to learn
people dont listen any more

cant sit down with open mind
open heart. he yearned for us
the young ... to carry on
original ways of this land
have faith ongwehonwe
a man with no enemies
a man of the earth
a man who yearned for us, the young
People, with each elder's passing
youd think we'd learn, to be One
is to be the child who learns
the strong & able ones who protect & provide
the elders who teach
a life without one
is a life incomplete

what is the tall & strong corn
without the many sorts of beans
    growing up cornstalks
& what are these without the squash
    close to the earth, protecting the roots
    a hard, weathered face but so bountiful
    in fruit inside . . .
people; let us nourish & protect each other

Stone Song (Zen Rock) The Seer & the Unbeliever

Why did i let things go this far?
  The rock starts its journey when the earth heaves.
I shouldve known how it would end.
  The rock splits along the way, different paths it will take.
How couldve i changed things?
  The rock moves along its ride, anyway it can, anyhelp offered,
  any obstacle will matter little, knows rock.
What can i do to set things right?
  The rock knows not, how can it, it stays, it moves, it splits,
  its song the same, only who hears it differs.
How will i continue, what next plan, i must know, i must make things happen.
  Rock remembers every color, animal, light & dark, every shudder unseen yet it
  carries no burdens. Every knowing song from another creature-force will also
  remember the shape that rock had taken in its vision, its place, how wind
  carved it or curved round it, yet the memory is no burden, it is only a song
  sung at the right time, forever to be heard. Never to be lost.
I will do better next time.
  Rock doesnt lie, the journey never ends, only is & is again.
I am a better man for this.
  Rock can be the weapon, the healer, is only there at that only time for that

124

only purpose, is used & used again, it has no memory of that event to burden it, the memory & reason belongs to another, Changed or Changer, rocks path is unchanged.

Now i gotta deal with yesterdays bizniz (before i go on).

Rock sings, its scars shine, chips left behind-each as important as the Path, the Ride, the endless journey, the Constant Unknowing-knowing well.

Rock can laugh.

So much unfinished bizniz.

Rock goes on, wearily in knowledge; knowledge a hollow, a shape, someone elses memory, rock is forever propelled by others, someplace to stop if the song is unsure or somehow unwise, rock is spread out even further than its wake of chips, yet never will stop; how can it?

This moment, give me relief.

Rock sweats when held, rock bleeds when cast, rock shines when found,
rock obscures when placed inside, rock marks when left behind,
rock never was when never seen, rock is the hollow in the shape of events.
(ignorance is a passingthing, quick to stand yet no base to sit, the earth moves
the song is changed, rock turns to stone with edges removed & can stay for ages
just so,a pleasant song,yet inside stone will turn to rock,edges return to pierce
the song, to escape as if never held)

I need relief, help, remorse, (is this pity?).

Rock gives & never takes; only in the roundabout song, the song that returns & is taken back only to give or be given away; never keep it-such songs burden & rock is Will, & can be Hard.

I give this moment away, i go on, in hope.

Rock hears but is circled by all, it can not help but hear.
Hope is a human thing: frail, weak, blinding, untouchable,
a bunch of chips held in a pouch, held with spit & human glue.

I give. I go.

Rock becomes chip, becomes stone, becomes song, returns, is the Path,
is the Ride, is the Journey, is the dream & the Maker, where once it ended
now returns, a drop into the ocean, a flash into the depths, a curving song
that laughs & plays & sends up bubbles to mark its path, they burst up into air,
hollows & space & shapes & whispers, instant faces . . . gone.

I return.

The stone starts a journey when the earth heaves. Turns to rock. Over & over.
The rock finds a path, a path that sings, any path for all paths sing.

THE FACE . . .

THE FACE. . . they called him The Face
not the Two Face, the trader, the agent
but Face Within the Face
like Bear testing the Wind
like Snake whispering to that someone
   over your shoulder
like Wolf staring at the eye behind your eye
   from across the dewey field before he melts
     among the redsticks into the Dark Green aroma

The Face no one knew where it had come from
to visit this person but
He came this person the People came to appreciate in an old way
Never swearing this Hard Face
Never laughing easy at anothers troubles
they say he would laugh when winds howl & cry
and Danger would not stay Observed thru his Tigers Eye
Danger would melt into the Dark Dark mist

Never looking down at the unfortunate, the displaced the dispassioned
Never looking up to ritual respect of man-made things, the paper &
               the glue of human evolution
Always straight ahead his gaze the clearest lake the hardest stone
the brightest fire dying down to warm embers that becalm the night of
                         Darkest Darks
                         & shaking dust

Never deflected
Never hidden
his hand one motion from those eyes his hands would say it all
like the cutting blade removing the rot from fruit:
This Once Was Mine Now I Give To You
You who chatters as the littlest furred tree climber
You who looks from place to place, looking for lost things
   not even remembering What shape? What color?
You who enjoys to play with Things: collecting, stacking, storing, hanging
   & wrapped round your neck, driving you here & there with your circle of keys
   opening & unopening, locking & unlocking, emptying to fill again
You busy as the beaver, even as unknowing building the damn that leads to the flood
You inheritor
You blood of my blood
You the long remembered wave that sent boats & boats of fishermen out upon
   the current, now returns a pitter & patter to slap against a rotted pier
   See that sleek new boat of glass, all motor, all power, yet
   he must seek shelter from the large waves of laughing
   & oil spluttering boats of consequence
You uninterested observer

You   wherein the Nation lies awaiting to awaken
        a tingle in your groin, a passing fancy, a wonder "what if?"
you   that silly face one day will turn to stone
        with only a crooked smile to remember
        how once it was
        & how it has
        Changed
        upon the Rivers
        of Human Dreaming
        Again.

"Dead Heroes"

There are no heroes
you are the light of your soul;
the ones who give us heroes
also say we have no souls,
i guess its a switch
inside our heads,
you can't turn it on
until your plugged in

to the diggers   who
& drowners   use
& dammers   air/water/land
& drillers   our grandchildren's
& refiners   medicines
& storekeepers   & leave wounds
& moneykeepers to heal with pills or cash
                        & the need for Security
                        Oh they promise Security
to protect ALL that you have accumulated.
Heroes are made when they
discard their baggage
and learn to survive
faster than they can think

and if the risk is too great
they die ... heroes do.

don't built your foundations
on another ones dreams
your search for the Big Place
the Longhouse of Hope & Light
will fall around
your ears that won't hear
your eyes that can't see

a time before
Boarding Schools became Mothers
Governments became Fathers
rules & regulations became
bratty siblings who we idolized
or despised in turn,
is that why we are aimless
and rebellious of authority
that comes from papers:
receipts for goods taken
invoices for bills paid
treaties for land stolen
bad health for trust
& the risk of survival
the willing risk we let go
to become dependent &
enjoy the solitary grace
of complaining?

"Let us use our grandchildren's medicines
so they can give their grandchildren the
accumulations of our rushing generation,
so bright the lights that guide us, we
forget our lonely souls, surely these
future young will one day find
our souls for us and forgive us
as loving children will, surely
good shall come of it . . . in time."

who speaks this? knowingly?

it is not "if our souls exist"
but is the futures gain
worth this present risk
we who travel heavy with
the burdens we willingly
placatingly   accept?

with open eyes & closed hearts . . .
when the blood pumps
for tomorrows seed
why must we forsake the thirsty land
& all earthly companions
that might have taught
our grandchildren
how to become
humans

again

(lost, humans are,
searching for what their
wise men say no longer exists
sacrificing worthless wealth
to bask in the flame of a
shooting star
we lovingly call
hero)

Photo by Paul Rosado (1982)

Maurice Kenny

"Spawning"

Mid-June, summer solstice, and my needs to return/home itch my fin/foot, my wing/arm. I fear I am salmon whose instincts demand a return to the natal waters up-river for the life cycle. Winters I hibernate in the city, enjoying the mild cold and rare snow fall, but at first thaw when legs feel maple sap run shoes become heavy, shoulders droop from holding overcoats. Crocus grow in my Brooklyn neighborhood in a stranger's cemented yard safe from April-hungry rabbits. When greeted by the yellow or purple petals I feel the first rumblings and shiverings of spring commence in my veins. Blood tightens. Arms wriggle in the cocoon knowing red trilliums open in north woods, that deer nibble new shoots, and Ray Fadden's Adirondack bears have edged towards the granite rock seeing the suet he never fails to put out. By then raccoon has scented old garbage, red-tail has climbed to a high elm, struggling with leaf-buds, in search of mice come from winter burrow. I know blackberry brambles creep up slate walls fencing cows from newly planted corn, and strawberry vines spread down sloping meadows and edge lanes in grasses reaching higher and higher under the sunlight.

I should say how important, and why, the wild strawberry is. It is the first natural fruit of the eastern spring. It is also the symbol of life to Iroquois people. It is important in traditional ceremony. My childhood was spent wandering from patch to patch behind my mother and sisters. My knees have bent, and my back has been broken in those long meadows, but my tongue sweetened. I now offer my adowe, a personal thanks, and hope for its continued growth and survival. I learned much in those northern fields under skies carved by birds and clouds and

129

winds: *thanks, respect, the importance of the family circle, the value of honest labor, the pleasures and the essential beauty of the natural, and the need to preserve and protect not only what is useful and beautiful, but all that the Creator placed on this earth to endure. The two-legged, human beings, are wont to forget the totality of the Creator's gift, and in their egotism seem to almost deplore the right to survival of the other creations.*

For me it is of the utmost importance to touch earth, the earth where the berries grow, bleed into the soil re-newing life. It is a re-newal, continuum; a symbol of my being and all beings, an image of my life and all life. Wendy Rose once presented me with a Christmas card she drew and painted, a drawing of myself sitting atop a huge red strawberry. It hangs on my bedroom wall both a compliment and an emblem.

So I travel home/north to the re-birth of chicory, burdock, tadpoles, otters and the strawberry. I fly with geese who, like myself, have wintered in a more southern clime, or salmon who have matured in the ocean. I travel home to those natal waters. "Home" is with your people who stand on that earth and partake of its nourishment, spiritual and corporeal. And though some, like yourself, have wandered they too cannot refrain from returning picking time. Once fingers have been lowered to the earth they cannot be retracted.

> *"My fingers in the earth ... I could see*
> *I could hear ..."*

Hopefully, I will go back to Brooklyn with not only a few jars of jammed berries, but with newly spawned wings, new legs, a bear poem, and a fresh song of thanks and praise, my imperative urge, needs satisfied, re-newed for another season.

Going Home

The book lay unread in my lap
snow gathered at the window
from Brooklyn it was a long ride
the Greyhound followed the plow
from Syracuse to Watertown
to country cheese and maples
tired rivers and closed paper mills
home to gossipy aunts ...
their dandelions and pregnant cats ...
home to cedars and fields of boulders
cold graves under willow and pine
home from Brooklyn to the reservation
that was not home
to songs I could not sing
to dances I could not dance
from Brooklyn bars and ghetto rats
to steaming horses stomping frozen earth
barns and privies lost in blizzards
home to a Nation, Mohawk
to faces I did not know
and hands which did not recognize me
to names and doors
my father shut

Wild Strawberry

For Helene

And I rode the Greyhound down to Brooklyn
where I sit now eating woody strawberries
grown on the backs of Mexican farmers
imported from the fields of their hands,
juices without color or sweetness

>   my wild blood berries of spring meadows
>   sucked by June bees and protected by hawks
>   have stained my face and honeyed
>   my tongue...healed the sorrow in my flesh

>   vines crawl across the grassy floor
>   of the north, scatter to the world
>   seeking the light of the sun and innocent
>   tap of the rain to feed the roots
>   and bud small white flowers that in June
>   will burst fruit and announce spring
>   when wolf will drop winter fur
>   and wrens will break the egg

>   my blood, blood berries that brought laughter
>   and the ache in the stooped back that vied
>   with dandelions for the plucking,
>   and the wines nourished our youth and heralded
>   iris, corn and summer melon

>   we fought bluebirds for the seeds
>   armed against garter snakes, field mice;
>   won the battle with the burning sun
>   which blinded our eyes and froze our hands
>   to the vines and the earth where knees knelt
>   and we laughed in the morning dew like worms
>   and grubs; we scented age and wisdom

>   my mother wrapped the wounds of the world
>   with a sassafras poultice and we ate
>   wild berries with their juices running
>   down the roots of our mouths and our joy

I sit here in Brooklyn eating Mexican
berries which I did not pick, nor do
I know the hands which did, nor their stories...
January snow falls, listen...

Corn-Planter

I plant corn four years:
ravens steal it;
rain drowns it;
August burns it;
locusts ravage leaves.

I stand in a circle and throw seed.
Old men laugh because they know the wind
will carry the seed to my neighbor.

I stand in a circle on planted seed.
Moles burrow through the earth
and harvest my crop.

I throw seed to the wind
and wind drops it on the desert.

The eighth year I spend planting corn;
I tend my fields all season.
After September's harvest I take it to the market.
The people of my village are too poor to buy it.

The ninth spring I make chicken-feather headdresses,
plastic tom-toms and beaded belts.
I grow rich,
buy an old Ford,
drive to Chicago,
and get drunk
on Welfare checks.

They Tell Me I Am Lost

For Lance Henson

my feet are elms, roots in the earth
my heart is the hawk
my thought the arrow that rides
        the wind across the valley
my spirit eats with eagles on the mountain crag
        and clashes with the thunder
the grass is the breath of my flesh
        and the deer is the bone of my child
my toes dance on the drum
        in the light of the eyes of the old turtle

my chant is the wind
my chant is the muskrat
my chant is the seed
my chant is the tadpole
my chant is the grandfather

and his many grandchildren
        sired in the frost of March
        and the summer noon of brown August
my chant is the field that turns with the sun
        and feeds the mice
        and the bear red berries and honey
my chant is the river
        that quenches the thirst of the sun
my chant is the woman who bore me
        and my blood and my flesh of tomorrow
my chant is the herb that heals
        and the moon that moves the tide
        and the wind that cleans the earth
            of old bones singing in the morning dust
my chant is the rabbit, skunk, heron
my chant is the red willow, the clay
        and the great pine that bulges the woods
        and the axe that fells the birch
        and the hand that breaks the corn from the stalk
        and waters the squash and catches stars
my chant is a blessing to the trout, beaver
        and a blessing to the young pheasant
            that warms my winter
my chant is the wolf in the dark
my chant is the crow flying against the sun
my chant is the sun
        sleeping on the back of the grass
            in marriage
my chant is the sun
        while there is sun I cannot be lost
my chant is the quaking of the earth
        angry and bold

although I hide in the thick forest
        or the deep pool of the slow river
        though I hide in a shack, a prison
        though I hide in a word, a law
        though I hide in a glass of beer
            or high on steel girders over the city
            or in the slums of that city
        though I hide in a mallard feather
            or the petals of the milkwort
            or a story told by my father

though there are eyes that do not see me
        and ears that do not hear my drum
        or hands that do not feel my wind
        and tongues which do not taste my blood

I am the shadow on the field
        the rain on the rock
        the snow on the limb
        the footprint on the water
        the vetch on the grave
I am the sweat on the boy
        the smile on the woman
        the paint on the man

I am the singer of songs
        and the hunter of fox
I am the glare on the sun
        the frost on the fruit
        the notch on the cedar
I am the foot on the golden snake
I am the foot on the silver snake
I am the tongue of the wind
        and the nourishment of grubs
I am the claw and the hoof and the shell
I am the stalk and the bloom and the pollen
I am the boulder on the rim of the hill
I am the sun and the moon
        the light and the dark
I am the shadow on the field

I am the string, the bow and the arrow

December

Set up the drum.
Winter's on the creek.

Dark men sit in dark kitchens.
Words move in the air.
A neighbor is sick.
Needs prayer.

Women thaw frozen
strawberries.

In the dark. . .a drum.

        Kids hang out
        eating burgers
        at McDonalds.
        The Williams boy
        is drunk.

Set up the drum.

Berries thaw,
are crushed,
fingers stained, and tongues.

Set up the drum.
A neighbor is sick.
Say a prayer.
Dark men sit in dark kitchens.

Wind rattles the moon.

Photo by Joseph Bruchac

Tauhindauli / Frank LaPena

TAUHINDAULI (Frank LaPena) of the Wintu-Nomtipom. Painter, photographer, sculptor, poet, writer, presently Director of Native American Studies and Associate Professor of art California State University, Sacramento. Author of two collections of poetry: The Gift of Singing *and* Sunusa Stopped the Rain. *Anthologized in* CALAFIA. *His work has appeared in* Contact II *and* From the Center. *Tauhindauli has read in California primarily and is in the PBS TV production* "California Indian Performing Arts". The Legends of the Yosemite Miwok *is a recent work. His art works have appeared in numerous shows and galleries in the United States, Europe, Cuba, and South America.*

"My most meaningful education has been from the medicine people, singers, and elders of my tribe as well as other northern California Indian tribes and other Indian people."

There was a time when the stars fell like rain. It was in the year of 1833. The Wintu tribe speak of this time in reference to our last battle with the Shasta tribe from the north; and they talk of the consequences of that star fall.

Around the time
of the "falling stars"
the Shasta were defeated
for the last time
by the Wintu

On the ridge at
the western rim
Widemcanus killed
the Shasta war leader
with the yellow throat

"Look" the storyteller said
"it went from here"...
his fingers traced
the jawline, under
the chin and down
the throat

Many Shasta were killed
and later death
turned and came
to the Wintu

The malaria epidemic
of 1833 killed 75%
of the people and
those left were overwhelmed
by the numbers of the dead
they could only sorrow
in the grief

The smell of death filled the air
forcing survivors to burn
or leave the bodies unburied.
A village became known
as "stench flesh"
because it was impossible
to bury the rotting bodies

It was a hard
and difficult time
We remember it
as the time
of falling stars

I Am Stone of Many Colors

I am stone of many colors
some colors heal
while others
speak of madness

My surface is mirror
to the universe
and just causes
turned to sand
but still existing
feeling rain, and sun
and wind

We must always remember
we are sacred
our messages
hidden by lost
references and symbols

Like man
we are
eternal in one sense
vulnerable in the next

Wrapped Hair Bundles

The birds turned
stopping
the flow of things
reminding me of
dream times
hair cutting times
when grief wraps
small bundles
of hair

It's all right
to stop and shake
his hand
How are things, "Peeny"

Trying to show how
things really are
His father cuts
his hair
in a shawl of white
and he in turn
has his hair cut

For bundles
to show
how death takes
gifts of hair
and makes
itself a shawl

The Year of Winter

The image of earth
in winter
is what is remembered
with grey sage figures
showing here and there

Winter gave them ice
river roads
and people moved then
on the bones of Winter
ribbon highways

The rivers were crossed
and recrossed
by wading people
going for riverbanks
that vanished in the spring thaw

Silent as guide
column stones
the people sat
like stacked stones
upright in the
spring melt

An elder hugged the skull
of his ancestors and weeped
openly and unashamed

The sweet smell of flesh
was coming alive
with the melting snow

The earth was covered
with the bones of winter
for as far as the eye could see

Waiting for a Second Time

my friend cannot speak any more
but he knows everything we say
and everything we're thinking
he had a stroke and fell
and was found wandering around
like a bloodied punchdrunk fighter
trying to make things right again

I saw him on the second day
with tubes of saline juice
feeding him moisture
which he never wanted or cared for
his body protested
being immobilized in his metal bed
though the stroke guaranteed
a certain immobility
he was tied down to
"insure his safety"

I looked into his eyes
and recalled the times
we talked about getting old
and how "a damned shame
it was to fall down, break arms
and legs and lose the ability
to keep a good hard on"
"it's hell on the woman, it's
hell on the man," old age even
stopped one from remembering
what herb to take
for such disorders

I hoped he remembered those
stories for they had that humorous
side only the afflicted can appreciate
the nurse complained he never
ate for them but did for us
as she gave him his potassium
in tomato juice

the heart medicine uses up the
body's supply of potassium
and orange juice and tomato juice
are used to ease its bitterness
if getting old is to lose one's
taste, potassium reminds
the patient he is
very much alive
and the laugh is still on him

for several days he talked
to us with hand signs
and all of us got frustrated
by the lack of understanding
our separating worlds forced
upon us

he wanted to know how long
he had been there
would he be able to talk again
and see, he pointed to each side of his mouth
biting his fingers
first on one side
and then the other
it was difficult to eat
and some jello dribbled out to
prove his point

we joked with him and his nurse
with a reminder to her to be agile
because you never know about
an instantaneous cure for
coyotes, in the meantime be sure
to come in on the right side
and stay away from the left

later, he came to me
in a dream
cleared his throat
and spoke
I was so surprised
and pleased for him
I forgot to listen
to what he was saying

I stay away
from hardline guessing
do my dreaming
in a light state
and wait for him
to tell me
a second time
for emphasis

Photo by Barbara Littlebird

Harold Littlebird

Born in Albuquerque, New Mexico, Harold Littlebird is a Pueblo Indian from the pueblos of Santo Domingo and Laguna in New Mexico. A 1969 graduate of the Institute of American Indian Arts, where he won the Vincent Price Poetry Award, his time is devoted to two major fields of art, pottery and writing. A guest poet and performer at many schools and universities, he was included in a 1972 documentry of living American Indian craftsmen and artists produced by Sveriges Radio-TVF 2, Stockholm, Sweden, and his poetry translated into the Swedish language. He is the subject of a videotape from the University of Arizona, SONGS OF MY HUNTER HEART, LAGUNA SONGS AND POEMS, which is part of their Native Literature from the Southwest series. A guest performer at the Opening Ceremonies of the Sundance Film Institute in Sundance, Utah, he also appeared in The Sun Dagger, *a film about the Chaco Canyon Solstice marker. The author of a book of poetry which is illustrated by his own drawings, ON MOUNTAINS BREATH (Tooth of Time, 1982), his work has appeard in numerous literary magazines, including* Alcheringa, The New York Quarterly, *and* The Greenfield Review. *He lives in Taos, New Mexico.*

If You Can Hear My Hooves

if you can hear my hooves in crisp autumn leaves
see my blue-grey body of winter
then you will know the song in my heart
songs of my hunter heart
pulsing steadily with my eyes
awaiting the deer dancing with my spirit
pray there is that strength in me to bring him home

Coming Home in March

partying by a river near Ellwood City, Pennsylvania
getting loud and high
keeping company with people I met
empty cans of past party-ers and broken glass
a song from numbed mouth coming out
weakly bouncing back through the quiet
we all stood by the tracks and laughed at my song
"hey little Indian, sing that again"
"yeah bird, again"
song building
louder, clearer
"that's far-out, man"
"you're all right, Littlebird, right-on"
"yeah far-out, bird"
... away in winter
when men of the pueblo, young and old
sing the season, and the village echoes the heart throb
of the drum beating strong ...
a wind in the trees
moon climbing high
stars shining brightly through cloudless sky
singing my heart deep into the night
holding on, remembering
lump in my throat growing harder

Hunter's Morning

I went out only once with my bow last year
high into the scattered snow mountains above Vallecitos and
did not get a deer but caught the before sunrise chill on my face
felt my weight break the still-frozen snow beneath my feet
looked back to see my prints just visible in the coming light
smelled a cool wetness of clear springs trickling in the dark
saw the outlines of tall ponderosa pine with ice-bent branches
quietly rustling in the wind's soft breathing as I climbed
still higher
stopped to catch my breath and heard two far-off crows caw
for the coming sun and was audience to coyotes barking
back and forth between unseen canyons
watched the blue-grey sky lighten and silent stars fade
felt cold Winter breezes numb my face while I sat shivering
on a rocky ledge overlooking a dim and hazy horizon
blew warm breath into my cupped hands and looked and listened
attentive, while the sun, now rising
cast patches of red and yellow light on distant blue mountains
walked as quietly as I could through dry scrub oak thickets
looking for fresh tracks and droppings in the calm splendor of dawn
began to feel that warm glow run all through me
stopped and prayed, whispering gratitude for that one hunter's morning
held in memory

A Circle Begins

in the surround of snow-touched mountains
a circle begins
in a meadow by a snow melt creek
where hands weave a house of thin green saplings
            it is a way of song
            a way of breathing
a pure womb to center oneself through sweat
a way of blessing and being blessed
a circle of humility, prayer and asking
and there are no clocks to measure time
but the beating of our singing hearts

After the Pow-Wow

(an excerpt)

I tell him how it used to be in Paguate
before the Jackpile Uranium mine opened,
the way my mother remembers it
She would say: *"That's when there was still farming*
through the valley and on up the canyon;
the peach trees and rows of corn, melon patches and
fields of grain and wheat where the mine is now.
That was when it was still a long ways from the village."
And how she said not too many Paguate men worked there yet,
now it is an ugly scar just east of the village
across the two-laned highway
And the mill tailings are left uncovered,
blown about by the winds,
with no provisions for removal and no one in authority
seems to care.
How the people were told to build the foundations of their
new houses with the tailings and how they used this excess
to line the roads to hold the dust down
In the community buildings where some ceremonies are held,
the dirt floor is mixed with these tailings.
Now there are more cases of cancer, birth defects and
internal disorders in the elderly;
and more up-dated statistics on how to get more uranium
with modern equipment brought in by large oil companies
like Exxon, Shell, Amoco.

The People are caught in a catch-22
They have to work in order to live, and the mine is there,
the money keeps coming, and the people keep working
under unhealthy and dangerous conditions;
and so the songs will continue.
It's not his fault I know, so I sip my coke and
change the subject
and we continue to talk about traveling
but I will remember to sing for him also.

The preceding excerpt is taken from a narrative describing a chance conversation which took place in the
Los Angeles International Airport, between myself and a representative of a large oil company with
mineral holdings in New Mexico. I was returning from a Pow-wow in Davis, California.

144

Adrian C. Louis

BIO: *Born 1946 Lovelock, Nevada of Paiute mother and Spanish father. Father ditched me at age one, grew up with skins on Indian land. Am enrolled, etc. Left Nevada at age of 21 for ten years in American time tunnel of Kerouacian influence. Spotty education, BA in AmLit and MA in Writing So Creatively from Brown University in Rhodieland. One-time Ph.D. candidate at U. of Nevada in Reno. Long time used to log each poem published but quit several years back—four chapbooks published. Have recently discovered higher plane of journalism—since March '82 have been editor of* Talking Leaf, The Los Angeles Indian Newspaper.

POETIC: *Modern art (poetry) is primarily precious, serving only the ego of the artiste. Poets (especially* Indin *poets) should use their tool of words for political gain and cultural survival. White world poetry is a dying art form, having reached its peak with W. B. Yeats. Indian poets must keep us from dying as a culture, as a race—too many skin bards are writing about coyotes and turtles when they should be writing about their brothers and sisters who have murdered their livers. We should be writing about the children born of relocation, about urban skins and res poverty, about the continual termination policies of this gov't, about 49's and snagging, about our strengths as members of specific and autonomous nations, those things we call recognized tribes. I say this for all my relations.*

The Hemingway Syndrome

Lovelock, Nevada—June 3, 1980

A friend drops me at   Indian Cemetary
several miles outside of town.
I smoothe   small waves of sand that
have drifted against   markers of blood:
Grandmother   Grandpa Joe   uncle Melvin   and
my nameless older brother born dead.
Years have deadened me beyond grief yet I
think   the only absence under the baked
and rocky soil: my mother buried two
hundred miles to the South.
I shoulder my backpack   march toward
the South   the pragmatic   purple mountains

Stopping randomly to shoot at lizards
I hike hours past roads.
Tinctures of blooming June desert
are quickly blackening   I stumble
upon a bleached-board shack.
Unquestioning night must be shut outside.
I light a fat   red candle
bitch-bound in an emptied bourbon bottle.
The cheap wax runs like sacrificial blood
      pools upon the hard   dirt floor.
Unable to penetrate it curdles
as cold as remembered lips.
I seduce my second pint of liquor.

In the lapping light shapes change.
My loaded backpack   an ex-lover
back turned   the love we shared.
My rifle   a vile   black snake
      my rolled sleeping bag   a napalm cannister.
By wavering candlelight the one book I
brought is finally impossible to read.
One page of Henry Adams   a recurring vortex
of infirm   cowardly words.
Having read enough I pave a circular path
around the large room   wish for a t.v.
Bored   I grab my rifle   do army routines:
Present arms   open the breech for inspection.
I despise myself for such weakness.
My fingers twitch
      I touch my groin.

Elegy for the Forgotten Oldsmobile

July 4th, 1981 and all is Hell.
Outside my shuttered breath the streets bubble
with flame-loined children in designer jeans
looking for people to rape or razor.
A madman covered with running sores
is singing on the street corner:
"Oh beautiful for spacious skies ..."

The landscape is far too convenient
to be either real or metaphor.
In an alley behind a milk store
a Black pimp dressed in Harris tweed
preaches fidelity to two pimply whores
whose skin is white   though they are not quite.

Crosstown in the sane precincts of Brown University
bearded scientists are stringing words
outside the language   inside the guts of atoms.

Uncle Adrian! I'm in the reservation of my mind.
Chicken bones in a cardboard casket
meditate upon the linoleum floor.
Outside my door stewed   sinister winos
snore in a tragic chorus.
The snowstorming television is their mother.
Outside my window on the ledge of a flophouse room
ice wraiths shiver   coat my final cans of beer.
Where do the souls of Indian sinners fly?
Uncle Adrian ... you're dying—cirrohsis of the liver.
A first team all-state halfback in 1944.
I have a photo of you in your Lovelock
letterman's jacket—two white girls on your arms.

Nothing is static. I'm in the reservation of
my mind. Embarrassed moths unravel my linen
thread by thread asserting insectival lust.
Naked I'm a lonely locoweed in a barren city lot.
What are the options? Urban renewal? Skulking
      waiting to poison the final buffalo?

When I sing of the American night my lungs billow
Camels astride hacking appeals for cessation.
My mother's cigarette lighter inscribed:
"Stewart Indian School—1941" explodes in my hand
in elegy to Dresden   Antietam   Hiroshima
and Wounded Knee ... both Wounded Knees.
Uncle   this mad fag warrior nation is dying.
Our enemy   our ancestor's enemy is finally dying.
I guess we should be happy; dance with the spirit, but
I project regret to my high-school honey.

History has carried me to a place
where she has a daughter
older than we were when we loved.
She is the one whose mother wouldn't let her
marry me because of the Paiute blood in my veins.
Love needs no elegy but because of the baked-prick
possibility of the flame-white lakes of Hell
I will give one last supper
to the dying beast of need disguised as love
on deathrow inside by ribcage.
I have not forgotten the years
of midnight hunger   unlimited drugs
when I cried and held by pillow   muddled
in the melodrama of the immature.

Uncle Adrian . . .
I am in the reservation of my mind
and silence settles forever
the vacancy of my cheap city room.
In the wine darkness
my cigarette coal
tints my face Wovoka's shade.
I am in the dry hills in starshine
prone in shit-stained breeches
with a cold   blue rifle
waiting to shoot
the lean   learned cockroaches
who taught me to think and live in English.

Uncle Adrian . . .
You promised to give me
your Oldsmobile in 1962.
How come you didn't?
I could have had some
good times in high school . . .

Captivity Narrative: September 1981

Running   sweating   hair wet from the shower
I catch the train from Rockport to Boston.
Panting is hard for a recently ruptured heart.
This poor baby sits among pinstripes   trenchcoats
and slithers inside the *Globe*'s crossword puzzle.
A five letter word for mixed?
In my case it is blood. I am of two races.
Today every word in my mouth   death.
A religious ad on the printed page asks:
"Why do the heathen rage?"
I could give them Quasimodo's cage.
Old rain is driving against the train
    against honeysuckle captured in scent
by a blonde woman sitting next to me.
Her legs look like those I just lost.
I should rhyme something about the true cost.

How much better off would any poet be
if he she or it were a quadruple amputee?
I have all my limbs but sit in limbo.
A pitiful rain is driving against my heart
when a brown balloon floats into my office
with the proud and tired face
of the most beautiful woman I've ever seen.
A Chippewa from Ontario.
She bobs in the breeze of my questions
and bursts with my first lascivious regret
that I am now without a woman.
The brown balloon falls to the carpet
like a discarded condom.
A woman of flesh arises.
What have I done!
I scoop out a hole in my wet white soil
and bury an Indian heart. Colors converge.
The sun turns pink against a steel gray sky.
Lightning cracks   willow shadows
imprison the savage white world.
Her father with terminal cancer
just drank away his funeral savings.
He began coughing blood
    entered a coma   died.

I never wanted to be a Dianne Arbus.

Indian Education

Links   interwoven
the cold damn steel
the dungeon of philosophy:
that Nietzsche is peachy
suborns nostalgia.

Crumpled hidden soiled
and spoiled
the report card
in some recess
of my worn cloth mind
makes me reduce   seduce
remember when I read her letter:

My name is . . .
I am 38 years old and I got to school at . . .
I never went to school before
because I had to herd sheep. I asked
my father if I could go to school
but he said no I wanted to learn to read
and write and speak English so
I can get a job, I need to understand English
so I can talk to people I started classes
in January 1980 for the first time. now I
can speak some English and read an write I
can do some math too. I have five children.
I love school.

The Walker River Night

The Walker River night is pungent
with wildrose willow and   slaughterhouse.
I straddle   white highway dashes
like two fingers on the zipper
of a man too drunk to screw.
I am hiking into town
visiting my home after twelve years dozing
in the Holy Order of Objective Correlative.

But kin of my flesh Americans . . .
By the mere sheer fact
of these near fictive words
I exclude those of you
lucky enough to be unschooled.
You would not be summarily fooled
by the vortex of the image
by the canticles of Cain
by the worship of pain
or by one poor slob trodding
back to the Fourth of July.

And already the fireworks have started:
flame flowers rupture the black.
The great stone cloud   my mind
yearns for the chorus of ohhhs and ahhhs.

Ten miles from Yerington I shudder
while violin winds chide   buckbrush
     my balls shrivel in anticipation
of small town talk and touch.
And I wonder how I can tell them
that we exist before the artist's stroke.
That after the portrait we die.

I jam my hands into my pockets
and blank my brain to song.
From this valley soil
nearly a century ago
Wovoka Jack Wilson left
to sing the Sioux
the Ghost Dance
and tonight
we are returning together.

Photo by Elizabeth Woody

Phillip Yellowhawk Minthorn

I imagine, now, that it would be difficult speak of Poetry and the American Indian "Self". The Self where all poetry exists and arrives at and has always been a part of that proverbial dawn. I would say, "All of us are here, we are here . . . these voices wake within us; they would be aboriginal fish, ancient turtles rising up from the sea, ravens, flying at dusk . . . today, we are here . . . we must speak to one another."

A collection of his poetry, VIGIL OF THE WOUNDED, is being published this year by Strawberry Press.

Daybreak

If origin had lived in these birds,
These tired birds that leave this place

I would awaken
In a valley beyond myself

Where dust speaks of dust
Stone of stone,

A valley that does not measure memory
But light.

I would awaken
In the quiet breath of stories

The Animals tell of;

Of the first human beings,
Of a strange race of people that walk on two legs

And of a fear
That only the wind can cry and conjure of.

The Earth Cycle Dream

for a piece of the earth
he turns his eyes backwards
a thousand years
and lays them down on dry bones
coyote bones,
dreaming eyes turn white
in the long cycle of death
down beneath in his belly,
they are fossils
time-crusted
with sleep

for a piece of the earth
he becomes a blind man lost
asking the dead ones
for his eyes
but they cannot answer him
far beneath the earth
far below the return
of his own belly

for a piece of the earth
he becomes thirsty
with empty eye sockets
and cannot remember when or how old,
only the long ache
of throbbing roots
flowing upwards
around his decaying body
has now set him free,
he will let go

Vigil of the Wounded

past the blueing humus,
past the rooted bone
your shredded ache knows no end.

you spit moons, rinse the darkness of rage,
hollow out old graves in the deluge of certainty.
trembling, the generations call themselves back

to you. guided by the burning of stars
they trace the old passages,
follow the familiar odors of birth.

in the white light of the womb
you lead them stunned,
whispering, "sleep, my children, sleep"

night healing,
the spinning of the skulls forehead reveals sorrow.
naked, the ashes do not celebrate.

again, the fever of passion, the universal shudder
rings through the seasons.
the rituals of birth and death break the day

with sighs and a wound not yet healed.
time, your old friend, greets you in sympathy
and the multitudes of the ancients

weeping from their pollen hearts
hunger for your return.

From Which War

this night talk is godless
and no less a wailing,
a delirious thrust of birds
in the slit mouth of the naked heart, a blooming.
listen. blood is stirring in the moonless heat
and the soldiers are marching again,
their bones whistling Boots and Saddles in the grasses.
even the crickets are singing like mortals,
their sad little hymns of resurrection
beat oddly against the stars.

and somewhere there is god listening.
the dead swelling up in his ears,
petrified, crowding the coil
to the soul.

a hundred years, maybe, and they're still crazy.
the brilliant field, the skin I've crawled into
is a blinding sadness
and everytime I pull the burning trigger
I'm killing myself,
I'm killing my people all over again.
the pain is pure, too pure. my mouth
is a gun barrel that shoots both ways
and all I can do is to kiss myself
until I'm totally dead, totally believable.
I must love myself like that,
administering excuses through a two-bit straw
to shake the shackle, poison the lily hand,
unclot the sun dangling from the ceiling
and thrust some poor finger down my throat,
give up the chaos of teeth
that have been chewing and eating away
those light hearted versions of ancestry.

and now I see them gleaming like little moons
among the wounded
their deafening silence counting coup with the dead,
from which war I do not know
and I'm terrified.

This Earth

this Pacific ocean,
these spiraling forests

and the simple delicate maze of the shell:
vision? perhaps promise?

we believe
this life is not of any other

here, there is the untouchable
aboriginal fish in the air

their small alien profiles
beget sadness and blind the mind,

this extravagance is not of memory
but of a greater design,

though we had wanted to remember dearly

the truth
of all things,

we have entered these mountains
these rivers,

ourselves

and have found no imaginable miracle
but something of a powerful death,

the dreamer in his dream,
the unutterable songs caught in his throat

and the fierce light of the elements
that would move him to speak

be it of earth and only earth,
this fluted companion

whose infancy has made us
capable of love and terror,

though terror has brought us here
alone, abandoned from one another

we imagine love
by the memory of it

and begin not in beginings
but, first, in the teachings granted us

by those ancestral mothers and fathers
that we cannot fail

we cannot fail

this earth,
this arduous earth.

N. Scott Momaday

N. Scott Momaday, Kiowa poet, novelist, and essayists, was born in 1934 in Lawton, Oklahoma. He spent his childhood on various southwestern reservations where his parents worked with the Indian service, a period of his life chronicled in his autobiographical work THE NAMES (Harper and Row, 1977) and reflected in his Pulitzer Prize winning novel HOUSE MADE OF DAWN (Harper and Row, 1969). A graduate of the University of New Mexico, he received his M.A. and Ph.D. in English Literature at Stanford where he was a Creative Writing Fellow in Poetry. After teaching English and Comparative Literature for a number of years in Calforina at both Stanford and Berkeley, he returned to the southwest and is currently a member of the English Department at the University of Arizona. His other books include THE WAY TO RAINY MOUNTAIN (University of New Mexico Press), which tells the story of the migration of his Kiowa ancestors from northern Montana to the sputhern Plains and THE GOURD DANCER (Harper and Row), a collection of his poems. He is married and the father of three daughters.

The Delight Song of Tsoai-Talee

I am a feather on the bright sky
I am the blue horse that runs in the plain
I am the fish that rolls, shining, in the water
I am the shadow that follows a child
I am the evening light, the lustre of meadows
I am an eagle playing with the wind
I am a cluster of bright beads
I am the farthest star
I am the cold of the dawn
I am the roaring of the rain
I am the glitter on the crust of the snow
I am the long track of the moon in a lake
I am a flame of four colors
I am a deer standing away in the dusk
I am a field of sumac and the pomme blanche
I am an angle of geese in the winter sky
I am the hunger of a young wolf
I am the whole dream of these things

You see, I am alive, I am alive
I stand in good relation to the earth
I stand in good relation to the gods
I stand in good relation to all that is beautiful
I stand in good relation to the daughter of *Tsen-tainte*
You see, I am alive, I am alive

The Colors of Night

1. White

An old man's son was killed far away in the Staked
Plains. When the old man heard of it he went there
and gathered up the bones. Thereafter, wherever the
old man ventured, he led a dark hunting horse which
bore the bones of his son on its back. And the old man
said to whomever he saw: "You see how it is that now
my son consists in his bones, that his bones are polished
and so gleam like glass in the light of the sun and moon,
that he is very beautiful."

158

2. Yellow

There was a boy who drowned in the river, near the
grove of thirty-two bois d'arc trees. The light of the
moon lay like a path on the water, and a glitter of
low brilliance shone in it. The boy looked at it and was
enchanted. He began to sing a song that he had never
heard before; only then, once, did he hear it in his heart,
and it was borne like a cloud of down upon his voice.
His voice entered into the bright track of the moon,
and he followed after it. For a time he made his way
along the path of the moon, singing. He paddled with
his arms and legs and felt his body rocking down into
the swirling water. His vision ran along the path of light
and reached across the wide night and took hold of the
moon. And across the river, where the path led into the
shadows of the bank, a black dog emerged from the river,
shivering and shaking the water from its hair. All night
it stood in the waves of grass and howled the
full moon down.

3. Brown

On the night before a flood, the terrapins move to high
ground. How is it that they know? Once there was a boy
who took up a terrapin in his hands and looked at it
for a long time, as hard as he could look. He succeeded
in memorizing the terrapin's face, but he failed to see
how it was that the terrapin knew anything at all.

4. Red

There was a young man who had got possession of a powerful
medicine. And by means of this medicine he made a
woman out of sumac leaves and lived with her for a time.
Her eyes flashed, and her skin shone like pipestone.
But the man abused her, and so his medicine failed.
The woman was caught up in a whirlwind and blown
apart. Then nothing was left of her but a thousand
withered leaves scattered in the plain.

5. Green

A young girl awoke one night and looked out into the
moonlit meadow. There appeared to be a tree; but it was
only an appearance; there was a shape made of smoke; but
it was only an appearance; there was a tree.

6. Blue

One night there appeared a child in the camp. No one
had ever seen it before. It was not bad-looking, and it
spoke a language that was pleasant to hear, though none
could understand it. The wonderful thing was that the
child was perfectly unafraid, as if it were at home
among its own people. The child got on well enough,

but the next morning it was gone, as suddenly as it had appeared. Everyone was troubled. But then it came to be understood that the child never was, and everyone felt better. "After all," said an old man, "how can we believe in the child? It gave us not one word of sense to hold on to. What we saw, if indeed we saw anything at all, must have been a dog from a neighboring camp, or a bear that wandered down from the high country."

7. Purple

There was a man who killed a buffalo bull to no purpose, only he wanted its blood on his hands. It was a great, old, noble beast, and it was a long time blowing its life away. On the edge of the night the people gathered themselves up in their grief and shame. Away in the west they could see the hump and spine of the huge beast which lay dying along the edge of the world. They could see its bright blood run into the sky, where it dried, darkening, and was at last flecked with flakes of light.

8. Black

There was a woman whose hair was long and heavy and black and beautiful. She drew it about her like a shawl and so divided herself from the world that not even Age could find her. Now and then she steals into the men's societies and fits her voice into their holiest songs. And always, just there, is a shadow which the firelight cannot cleave.

The Fear of Bo-talee

Bo-talee rode easily among his enemies, once, twice, three—and four times. And all who saw him were amazed, for he was utterly without fear; so it seemed. But afterwards he said: Certainly I was afraid. I was afraid of the fear in the eyes of my enemies.

160

The Gourd Dancer

Mammedaty, 1880-1932

I. The Omen

Another season centers on this place.
Like memory the blood congeals in it;
And like memory, too, the sun recedes
Into the hazy, southern distances.

A vagrant heat hangs on the dark river,
And shadows turn like smoke. An owl ascends
Among the branches, clattering, remote
Within its motion, intricate with age.

II. The Dream

Mammedaty saw to the building of this house.
Just there, by the arbor, he made a camp in the
old way. And in the evening when the hammers had
fallen silent and there were frogs and crickets
in the black grass—and a low, hectic wind upon
the pale, slanting plane of the moon's light—
he settled deep down in his mind to dream. He
dreamed of dreaming, and of the summer breaking
upon his spirit, as drums break upon the intervals
of the dance, and of the gleaming gourds.

III. The Dance

Dancing,
He dreams, he dreams—
The long wind glances, moves
Forever as a music to the mind;
The gourds are flashes of the sun.
He takes the inward, mincing steps
Describing old processions and refrains.

Dancing,
His moccasins,
His sash and bandolier
Contain him in insignia;
His fan is powerful, concise
According to his agile hand,
And catches on the sacramental air.

IV. The Give-away

Someone spoke his name, Mammedaty, in which
his essence was and is. It was a serious matter
that his name should be spoken there in the circle,
among the many people, and he was thoughtful,
full of wonder, and aware of himself and of his name.
He walked slowly to the summons, looking into the
eyes of the man who summoned him. For a moment
they held each other in close regard, and all about
them there was excitement and suspense.

Then a boy came suddenly into the circle, leading
a black horse. The boy ran, and the horse after him.
He brought the horse up short in front of Mammedaty,
and the horse wheeled and threw its head and cut
its eyes in the wild way. And it blew hard and
quivered in its hide so that light ran, rippling,
upon its shoulders and its flanks—and then it
stood still and was calm. Its mane and tail were
fixed in braids and feathers, and a bright red chief's
blanket was draped in a roll over its withers. The
boy placed the reins in Mammedaty's hands. And all
of this was for Mammedaty, in his honor, as even now
it is in the telling, and will be, as long as there
are those who imagine him in his name.

The Eagle-Feather Fan

The eagle is my power,
And my fan is an eagle.
It is strong and beautiful
In my hand. And it is real.
My fingers hold upon it
As if the beaded handle
Were the twist of bristlecone.
The bones of my hand are fine
And hollow; the fan bears them.
My hand veers in the thin air
Of the summits. All morning
It scuds on the cold currents;
All afternoon it circles
To the singing, to the drums.

Photo by Mary Randlett (1982)

Duane Niatum

Duane Niatum was born in 1938 in Seattle, Washington. A Native American, he is a member of the Klallam Nation, whose ancestral lands are on the Washington coast along the Strait of Juan de Fuca. His early life was spent in Washington, Oregon, California, and Alaska, and at age seventeen he enlisted in the Navy and spent two years in Japan. On his return he completed his under-graduate studies in English at the University of Washington. He later received his M.A. from The Johns Hopkins University. He is currently teaching at Evergreen State College in Olympia, Washington.

Niatum's poetry has been published in The Nation, Prairie Schooner, American Poetry Review, The New England Review, and many other literary journals and anthologies. His previously published collections of poems are After the Death of an Elder Klallam, Ascending Red Cedar Moon, Digging Out The Roots, and Songs for the Harvester of Dreams. In 1973-74 he was the editor of the Native American Author series at Harper and Row, and in 1975 he served as the editor of Carriers of the Dream Wheel, an anthology of Native American poetry. He also writes and publishes short fiction, essays, and reviews.

It seems to me, when I feel closest to the Muse,
the most terrible reality beyond the knowledge
of my mortality is the first shock of recognition
that I am never the subject of the mirror, but
its object. And when I look out the window at
the view of the street and come to rest in the
remote pearl clouds, or later take a walk through
the nearby park lined with poplars, spruce, and
pine, and accidentally glimpse some bird riding
the current of the wind, appearing to follow
the path of the sunset to its origins—it is
the blazing colors of the sun, the flamboyant wing
curving a descent that soothes my quavering spirit
within, helps me to accept the natural order of
things—what I see, touch, taste, smell, and hear.
And it is this fusion of my imagination with
the body of the world that ultimately gives shape
and sound to my memory, redeems me from my own
arrogance or indifference.

> *——Duane Niatum*
> *Seattle, Washington*
> *January, 1983*

Street Kid

I stand before the window that opens
To a field of sagebrush—
California country northeast of San Francisco.
Holding to the earth and its shield of silence,
The sun burns my thirteen years into the hill.
The white breath of twilight
Whirrs with insects crawling down the glass
Between the bars. But it is the meadowlark
Warbling at the end of the fence
That sets me apart from the rest of the boys,
The cool toughs playing ping pong
And cards before lock-up.
When this new home stops calling on memory,
As well as my nickname, Injun Joe,
Given to me by the brothers,
The Blacks, the Chicanos, the others growing
Lean as this solitude, I step
From the window into the darkness,
Reach my soul building a nest against the wall.

Song from the Maker of Totems

I offer you the chance to forgive your wounds
That often burned down the longhouse.
And you must never blame the village shaker:
I comfort you because of his dreaming.

Watch owl settle in the four directions,
Roost in the fire that burns for salmon's way—
Circle First People who hide in your feelings,
To ease the weight of morning on your eyelids.

Hear the winds give away your pride
In confusion's cave, offer you a light burden,
Seven days of rain, and another storm.

Again, the water dreamers run away with hope:
Thunderbird because he's buried under bone,
Teeth, and shell; Raven because he can't see
Sun touch the crocus beneath the ferns;
Blue Jay because so few hear the humor in his

Laugh, his praise to the women who swim this river;
Whale because he's more hunted than haunted,
Seaweed because it's now mere desert dust.
Beaver because his last dam demolished

The rainbow that sent him off to the stars
Without a cedar chip to find his way home
When the water song fails to hold the summer storm.

Wolf roams the white pine of your terror,
But he'll stop when you stop running behind the dead,

The drummers behind the moon. At dawn, offer him
The wheel, the rattle to shake you to the shore;

It was your ignorance that started the tremor
That fed the sharks closing in;
The suicide stream inching its way to the breakers.

Chief Leschi Of The Nisqually

He awoke this morning from a strange dream;
Thunderbird crashed through the wall like a club.
And from the circle, Nisqually women led
him to their river, to dance to its song.

He burned in the forest like a red cedar,
his branches fanning blue flames toward
the white men claiming the camas valley
for their pigs and cows. Musing
over wolf tracks, the offspring of snow,
the memory of his wives and children
keeps him mute. Flickering in the dawn fire,
his faith grows grizzly, tricks the soldiers
like a fawn, sleeping black as the brush.
They laugh at his fate, frozen as a bat
against his throat. Still, death will take

him only to his father's longhouse,
past the rope's sinewy snap. These bars
lock in but his tired body; he will eat
little and speak less before he hangs.

Digging Out the Roots

Thirteen pieces of silver means bad luck,
If I think bad luck rolls thirteen ways,
And if I see the gambler, and not the forest.

Today I follow my spirit into the ruins
Of my Klallam ancestors, N'huia-wulsh,
Their white fir village, count the rainy seasons
Since grandfather fell in the brush like first cedar,
Where his flesh and bones settled in the dark
Regions of fern and snail. I return
To carve red moon out of my native sky.

Old Man canoeing on the Hoko river
Can mean much to a traveler who knows trouble
Is free and floating. Years and flights ago
This gentle grandfather, furious,
Struck me with a willow for defying him,
For fishing for rockfish that sang to agony
As I slapped their heads against the rocks.
The welts that appeared that blood-bright day
Are the songs embedded on my back and arms.

As a fern-shy boy in the Navy, I chained
Most of the voices of fear to coyote.
And as a minor drunk on legends from the sea,
I killed in delirium the Brig Warden
Who called me an idiot and a wetback.
But the ants of deliverance marched back into my blood
As those days shook me into manhood.

Home again, I meet a rare woman and we marry.
I watch her dry her thighs, by the yellow tub.
Her smile lights the walls with her dance,
The play of the kiss to dawn, and sleep.

We shared the labyrinths of two autumns,
Then, the scents of Seattle were alive,
Pine, rose, and maple, the sea a magic drummer,
Before the rain washed our dream out the window,
Leaving us two unknown statues.
The birth of a son our best poem.

Tossing the past back into the wine river,
I hid when the bottle crashed
Through the mirror and broke against my skull,
Before a new woman opened my eyes and I sighed,
When she whispered not to move,
So her hands could dance right down my back.

We painted our apartment light as the sun
Giving itself to a tahoma meadow;
Lived for its lake and swallows. I would
Carry her from the living room to our green bed,
Gently hold her warm breasts and body to my chest.

Neither she nor I remembered when or how the storm
Drove us far into the laughing mirror.
Having learned to love with irony,
We are careful and soft with the lights off.
Hearing music chip life otf the moon,
No one can tell us our flesh will not wrinkle
Like paper, our bones not crack
With the logs in the winter fire.

We hunted for a ring, from city to train,
Window to valley, mountain to stream,
Then the clouds passed, leaving the wind and us
On a hill in waves of Scotch broom.

Not quite ready to carry the silence wheel,
Another failure flamed down her cheeks
To find its home in my heart,
The day our shadows attacked us like flies,
Chasing us down the subway to the street.

On each night Trickster mocked my totems,
I pushed my fist into nightmare's eye,
The window clown who mimed each wound again.
But panic let me alone when she handed
The cottage key to the ghosts of my wife and son.
Memory burns away the confusion of naming.

Walking under the sun of budding flowers,
There seem to be fewer errors to trust,
Humility to tear, songs to puzzle cedar hawk's descent;
And by summer's end, perhaps ocher wind
Will keep these feathers for an open field.

Raven

The old ones whose ancestors hunted
the whale boast to the children
half listening of the chase they heard
when young, before an earlier dog salmon fire,

but the last canoe to skim water hangs
from the roof of the general store,
a relic dangling in obtuse space,
its myths as white as the storekeeper

who bought it for the somnambulant tourists.
Even he knows no one survives the rust
and spores of steel and concrete,
and if the Great Spirit ever spoke, it

must have been before his father or theirs.
Trapped in a dark he cannot fathom,
he watches for the owl that will pick
his bones as clean as the wind on the sea.

He sits down with the elders drinking
wine and chattering back to the chipmunk
racing across the woodpile for the night.
When silence consumes its chant,

Killer whale leaps near the river's mouth,
pounds the beach to a raven's caw.
With Snowberry woman but a photograph
in the window, the stories of mornings

elk, cougar, and beaver were seen
drinking the green dews of the Hoko
with the insects, glimmer only
in the light of the ashes.

Now the crier bearing the new season
to the village is the slow beat of the rain.
But once, when this rain turned to snow,
this snow to feathers, a voice

rose with a storm to sting the whalers:
"I am Kwatee, the Changer, your friend."
Fog Dreamer, the eldest singer, shook his
head and threw his rattle at the creature:

"You're too late, our children are gone."
He spit on the creature's black toes;
looked long at the mud slide of his longhouse.
Kwatee, alone, beat huge wings to stars.

Killer whale dove to ocean shadow and sky.
The old ones staggered off to sleep
the way the raven let them fall,
the way the fire cooled to coal.

Photo by Kirk Robertson

Nila NorthSun

i am a shosone/chippewa currently living on my reservation in fallon, nv. i am married to kirk robertson who publishes scree magazine. we have two children, amabese cody & bohabe jesse. for the time being i am 31 & unemployed. have a b.a. from the univ. of montana, missoula. grew up in the san francisco area. can't seem to grow vegetables & i don't like deer meat. i like to dance.

Publications: DIET PEPSI/NACHO CHEESE from Duck Down Press, P.O. 1047, Fallon, Nv. 89406. SMALL BONES, LITTLE EYES from Duck Down Press, with Jim Sagel. COFFEE, DUST DEVILS, & OLD RODEO BULLS published by Judson Crews with Kirk Robertson. AFTER THE DRYING UP OF THE WATER published by the Fallon Tribe, a tribal history.

Anthologies: The First Skin Around Me, A Geography of Poets, A Long Line of Joy, The Vagabond Anthology & two German anthos: American Freeway & Terpintine on the Rocks. A yet untitled book from Germany is forthcoming. And numerous small press magazines & newspapers.

170

falling down to bed

i used to look at with disgust
these indians laying around
on the dirt & grass
passed out drunk
their bodies littering
the pow wow grounds
or city parks
i'd look at their crumpled bodies
laying in the noon sun
still sleeping where
they fell
but one time
i went to the 49
after the pow wow
& got shit faced drunk
then got sleepy
& fell in the dirt parking lot
it seemed nice
the ground was clean in the darkness
the stars were vibrant above
the night air was cozy
'get up get up' they said
'no no leave me here
i want to sleep here'
luckily they shoved me into
the car
or i would have been
the drunk somebody looked at
with disgust
at least now
when i see them
i understand.

future generation

it was at a pow wow
teepees tents & trailers
were everywhere
arbors were set up
folding chairs tables
& coleman stoves
waiting silently in the
pre-dawn hours
it had been a good pow wow
lots of visiting exchanging news
the dancers were in good form
w/ some beautiful traditional outfits
standing out from the rest
the dancing went on till 2 that morn
& yet at dawn some people
were already stirring
grandpa crawled out of the tent
surveyed the sleepy encampment
& suddenly
he heard screams
from a nearby tent women & children
ran out screaming
grandpa thought of fire
or a teepee creeper
he ran over to help
little boys peeked back in the flap
so did grandpa
a wailing woman was
frantically unwrapping a baby
from a cradleboard
its mouth was full of white
lumpy stuff
& it did not move
grandpa hollered at
a man in there
'clear out the white stuff
start giving the baby
mouth to mouth resuscitation'
the man panicked
sucked the white stuff into
his own mouth
& started to choke
another woman tried
breathing into the baby
but its forehead was blue
& the still body was white
grandpa ran around camp
trying to find 'security' or a cop
he found one
they put the baby & mother in

the car & took off
the nearest hospital
20 miles away
but it didn't really matter
if it were 2 or 200 miles
the baby was dead
grandpa said it ruined
the whole pow wow for him
he kept thinking of
his own 8 grandchildren.

up & out

we total it up for
income tax
hoping to get a little
something back
but it seems we've moved ourselves
out of the poverty level
we made more money than
we've ever made before
but felt poorer
we made better money cause we
moved to the city
left the reservation where
there were no jobs
the city had jobs but
it also had high rent
high food high medical
high entertainment
we made better money but
it got sucked up by
the city by cable tv
by sparklettes water by
lunches in cute places
by drinking in quaint bars
instead of home like we did
on the reservation
there we lived in gramma's old house
no rent
the wood stove saved electricity &
heating bills
we only got one tv channel but
we visited with relatives more
there was no place to eat on the res
'cept a pool hall with chips & coke
there was only one movie house in town

& nothing good ever showed
we got government commodities that
tasted like dog food but
it was free
we got government doctors at i.h.s.
that graduated last in their class
but they were free
if a car broke down there was the
old pick-up truck or a cousin with
a little mechanical know-how
god how i hated living on the reservation
but now
it doesn't look so bad.

the sweat

the door closed
& we were there
sharing the darkness
sharing our prayers
sharing sensations when
the water hit hot rocks
these old women
with curled arthritic feet
shared their being
with the children who
gulped thirstily at
the dipper of water
even when the elders spoke
in their own languages
it didn't matter that
we couldn't understand
the feeling was there
the tragedy & agony & hope
so we cried with them
we shared that special time

& even after the door
was opened
& we slowly rose
adjusting our eyes to
the light outside
we knew when we saw
each other later
that glint of recognition
would remind us of
what we experienced
together.

the red road

tho he is young
his ways are ancient
tho no elder was there
to lead the way
his truths were
from the heart
therefore undisputable
as simple & as complicated
as the moon
the earth
the sun
as fragile as a seedling
but growing stronger with
a few well chosen words
from others who felt right
within themselves
he found strength
he found his way
onto the good road
tho there are those who
will doubt him
or his methods
none can question
the belief within himself
& only if he does
can he stray off the
red road
others cannot push him
from it
& as he goes
he beckons
& tries to make it easy
for others to follow
or at least
make them aware
it can be done.

Photo by Randy Thompson

William Oandasan

My tribe is the Ukono'um, more popularly known as the Yuki, of Round Valley in the coastal mountain ranges of northern California, approximately 185 miles north of San Francisco. We often are thought the oldest culture in existence on that section of the United States. We "seem" to have a unique culture land linguistic stock, and, like the famous California redwood trees, which were considered for the longest time to be the oldest, continuing life form in that region of the world, we have appeared as if to spring directly from the California earth more than 10,000 years ago. I have often thought, with much pride, of how long my ancestors must have lived in the redwood region to know that they were each the oldest representative of their respective kind and chose Ukono'um as our name, not Yuki, the name given to us.

My poems have been selected from Round Valley Songs, *a manuscript which is comprised of four songs of twelve verses that are four lines long, each song totalling 48 lines. Each verse and the lines of each verse are written in such a manner that they can be rearranged to become new, original poetic works. Consequently, many of the verse lines of* Round Valley Songs, *mainly in the song titled "Dreams," repeat themselves. This practice of rearranging lines and verses of old songs in order to create new songs has been a traditional native American cultural practice. I write poems with the idea that both work and play are involved in the creative process, simultaneously.*

When I write I want to communicate my expression in a concise, concrete image where form and content become extensions of each other with as little interference as possibly from myself. As a poet I wish to express my communication from where consciousness and unconscious synthesize with one another. Being a native American I must perpetuate and expand the cultural values of my tribe, my identity, through poetry. I am presently performing research in order to show that the creative process in which language is used to make poems and songs by early tribal and modern urban consciousnesses are essentially identical.

I am the editor of A, *a journal of contemporary literature, and the* American Indian Culture and Research Journal *(University of California at Los Angeles).*

176

Round Valley Reflections

"first there is the word
the word is the song"

1

song gives birth to
the story and dance
as the dance steps
the story speaks

2

in the chipped and tattered
weavings of a willow basket
the voice of an ancient age
dreaming of breath

3

long ago brown bears
sang around our lodge fires
tonight they dance
alive through our dreams

4

my eyes have closed
and look forward to sleep
but over fields, forests,
    mountains and clouds
i sail on an eagle's wing

5

with brilliant feathers and strength
three Pilipino gaming cocks
appear from across the water
in the yard pullets cluck excitedly

6

an emptied bottle of Coors
ditched in moonlight at Inspiration Point
mirrors the faces of drunkards
cold like snow

7

through the heart of Covelo
Commercial Boulevard parades past
a gas station, cafe, store, saloon,
    old barn
signs of the empire

8

"young and sound warrior
expand the ear of your mind
let my words paint visions
of tomorrow"   the brown owl said

"in an ancient Egyptian myth
the Phoenix rose from its ashes
   'from the ashes of the reservation
the People will rise again'

"may the rich brown clay, the feather
and foam, the marrow of our ways,
not be the ash of memory in print
but cold mountain water"

The Past

1

from heart through mind into image:
the pulse of the four directions
the voice of our blood
the spirit of breath and words

2

in chipped and tattered
weavings of a willow basket
the voice of an ancient age
dreaming of breath

3

in a chert arrowhead speckled with quarts
i have seen our grandfathers
along a stream east of the valley
lancing salmon and deer

4

swimming up the Eel
a spirit sings   *acorn-*
pound-the-old-way-draws
the-milk-of-Earth

5

from fresh currents of night air
above manzanitas near the cemetery
the words of ancient lips
turn in our blood again

6

a few traditions live
alongside a garden walk
in two large stones
now called mortar and pestle

7

for three days before and
after summer's new and full moons
beneath ripples near Dos Rios
bass will spawn near sandbars

8

long ago black bears
sang around our lodge fires
tonight they dance
alive through our dreams

9

when we spoke we spoke
the mother tongue of the valley
and counted the spaces between
   our fingers
today metrics cut under pounds,
   feet and quartz

10

the woman with white hair
only whispered   *Tatu*
but through my ears
30,000 years echo

11

skirmishes leading to blood and death
have marked the east ridges for centuries
but not one *just* killed before—
like at Fish Town on the South Fork!

12

on the summit of Black Butte
night wind races through long hair
and tears stream down laughing Yuki faces
tens of thousands of years old

William Oandasan   179

The Song of Ancient Ways

song gives birth to
the story and dance
as the dance steps
the story speaks

the woman with white hair
only whispered   *Tatu*
but through my ears
30,000 years drum

with brilliant feathers and strength
three Pilipino gaming cocks
appear from across the water
in the yard pullets cluck excitedly

swimming up the Eel
a spirit songs   *acorn-*
pound-the-old-way-draws
the-milk-of-Earth

free as the bear
and tall as redwoods
throb my blood roots
when spirits ride high

long ago brown bears
sang around our lodge fires
tonight they dance
alive through our dreams

in the chipped and tattered
weavings of a willow basket
the voice of an ancient age
dreaming of breath

the icy mountain water
that pierces the deep thirst
drums my fire
drums my medicine pouch

from fresh currents of night air
above manzanitas near the cemetery
the song of ancient ways
turns in our blood again

Photo by Pat French

Louis (LittleCoon) Oliver

I am an Oklahoman, a red man, as the name implies, yet my origins are somewhere along the Chattahoochee rivers which would be now in the state of Alabama. My people spoke the old Alabama language now practically extinct. Perhaps it is a fact that it was the oldest Indian language spoken in the history of the Muskogee of Creeks. Tho much of it is lost we speak a tongue similar to it. I'm proud of the few words I speak in Alabama, which is as old as the continent I live on. In all probability those old "bronze spatulas" that had the history of my people etched in Alabama are lost in the shifting sands of the Arkansas river and forever into the Great white waters. Only a vision could recall those words.

Actually my family name is Katcha or Tiger according to my line of Clanship. The United States Government agents did not understand fully the clan law and cared less, so they erred in recording our vital statistics. I am not that person the government so states that I am. I am happy to be that other person, who is of the golden Raccoon Clan of the old Indian town of Koweda, also partly of the Okfuskee town. Strangely, the Kowedas and Okfuskees spoke the same language, but there is a variation in the delivery and sound.

In my writing ventures I am part one person and part another showing some indications of a split personality. This came about in the attempted brainwashing (by the government) of our religion, culture and tradition, thru education.

181

I was born with a passion for the pastoral and idylic. Basically I'm a hunter and fisherman. I'm a free spirit when wandering thru the woods, wading the clear streams, climbing the mountains, crushing cedar and sage—filling myself with its aroma. Tho I have an affinity with the wild animals, the fowl of the air, the fish, the turtle, the gar—still I gaze in wonderment of them. I studied men and women both young and old. I took account of myself and found imperfections.

In my youth the white society tempted me with the apple of civilization and progress and I ate it to the core and now I know its dividends. Its path leads in two directions; one to wealth and power; the other to poverty and squalor. So, now I walk with only the Shell of the turtle, having been gutted, but retaining the stability of mind and spirit of my ancestors.

Now I am near four score years (the idea the Creeks had of aging was that a man was young and lithe at sixty or seventy)—so I am a Creek and a bit wiser.
Uotko-okisce!

Wagon Full of Thunder

Now—wagon full of thunder—
    wheels of great whisperings
    striking flint boulders—spitting
      white—blinding cold fire.
In the moon of great white winter
    the Horned Owl prophesied:
When Buffalo hump sizzles
    on the pole—dropping
    oily tears on coals sputtering
      then
Prepare for Thla-fo-thlako, the great winter.

Blackberry Bird told me then, too,
    speak the mystery words from
    great Conch shell—sing the songs
of the wind, the Turtle and the Gar
    that never die.
Burn cedar and white sage
    whose fragrance turn
    body inside out to free
    Spirit of wisdom.

Deer told me—get down low, low
    form circle of warrier friends,
    eat not the gizzards of fowls
    that you not die of thirst
      in battle,
    but savor the raw melt of us
      for he-man vigor.

I breathe on these wheels turning
    —things scratched on rocks
    so wind and bird may carry
to the ends of Odee, earth
Words off Indian tongue
    —from mind shell.

The Sharpbreasted Snake
(Hōkpē Fuskē)

The Muskogee's hokpi—
    fuski (Loch Ness
      Monster)
        Travelled here,
          by the Camp of
            The Sac and Fox;
              Thru the alluvial
                Gombo soil, flailing
                  Thrashing-up rooting
                Giant trees;
              Ploughed deep
            With its sharp breast.
          Come to rest by
          Tuskeegi Town, buried
        its self in a lake of
        mud to rest. The
        warriors of Tustanuggi
        were ordered to shoot
        it with a silver tipped
       arrow. With a great
      roar and upheaval The
      Snake moved on;
    winding by Okmulgee
    To enter (Okta hutcher)
  South Canadian River.
Thus his ploughed
  journey, The Creeks
  called (Hotchee
  Sufkel Deepfork
  River.
      One, Cholaka,
        observed The Snake
        had hypnotic Power.
          Could draw a person
           into a swirling.
              whirlpool. It
                made a sound
              Like a
                Tinkling
                silver
              Bell.
                  O
                    k
                      i
                      s
                    c
                  e.

Indian Macho

This black 'yeyhoo' said he's Seminole
   I bragged of being Creek 'injun'
      —tough guys, ya know—
tool dressers from the Seminole oil fields.
Pay-day and we hike for "Shanker" town-
There a makeshift bar—sawdust floor.
We don't know name brands of beer
We order two bottles of good ole "frogass"
Bartender say: "You mean, 'Progress', don't 'cha?"
We take table where Indian girl sits
She pays no mind—munching salted peanuts.
'Yeyhoo' told me she is 'cherry-kee'
"I know," he said, "she come from 'tally-kaw'."
Table too high or chair too low for her
—So her'boobs' were laying on the table
   seeming to look right straight at us
   reminding me of baldheaded beavers.
She listened to our 'bull' with her eyes.
After several round of 'speeded' beer
we began to 'show off' our manhood.
He took a bottle between his teeth—no hands
raised it straight up and emptied it.
We did an arm wrestle and he won.
I dropped a quarter for an excuse to
   look around under the table and saw
She sat spraddle legged on her chair
I came up saying: "good god!"
She paid no mind—just munched her nuts.
He flaunted a five dollar bill in her face
—burned it up with a lighted match.
I wrote a check for ten thousand dollars
—tore it to bits and pitched it in the air.
She leaned over and whispered: "You go with me."

Materialized into an owl.

Moonlight—fluorescently shining
      witches delight,
a night never to be forgotten.
We lay on pallets away from the house
      Telling tales that old ones told
—after telling we spit foor times
      Tuff Tuff-Tuff Tuff
      T'was the custom.

Not far away—old Indian burial
beyond it the wooded bottoms
        —a bewitched land,
Where 'este chupko' wanders
Striking trees with his whip;
Where little people live.

We hear screech owl far away
We have feeling of foreboding
        The owl comes nearer
        —now in tree top over us.
We turn pockets inside out
        To scare it away
but he makes laughing-cackling sounds
        dives down at us-snapping.
Old folks on porch whisper:
        'it is human"
We see owl on burnt snag,
My uncle shot the evil thing
He told us not to go and see.
As the sun came up, we all saw
        human entrails draped over snag.
Four days later—word came
        Old man Choska had died.

Empty Kettle

I do not waste what is wild
I only take what my cup
        can hold.
When the black kettle gapes
        empty
and children eat roasted acorns
        only,
it is time to rise-up early
        take no drink—eat no food
        sing the song of the hunter.
I see the Buck—I chant
I chant the deer chant:
        "He-hebah-Ah-kay-kee-no!"
My arrow, no woman has ever touched
        finds its mark.
I open the way for the blood to pour
        back to Mother earth
                the debt I owe.
My soul rises—rapturous
        and I sing a different song,
                I sing,
                I sing.

Photo by Mary Ann Lynch

Simon J. Ortiz

Simon Ortiz was born and raised in the Acoma Pueblo Community in Albuquerque, New Mexico, and schooled within the Bureau of Indian Affairs on the Acoma Reservation. He attended the University of Iowa where he enrolled in the International Writing Program and received a Masters Degree in Writing. In 1980, he was honored as a participant at the White House "Salute to Poetry and American Poets." He has authored numerous books: A GOOD JOURNEY, GOING FOR THE RAIN, FIGHT BACK: FOR THE SAKE OF THE PEOPLE, FOR THE SAKE OF THE LAND, HOWBAH INDIANS, and FROM SAND CREEK, his latest book, for which he won a 1982 Pushcart Prize. He has taught at San Diego State University and the University of New Mexico in Native American Literature and Creative Writing. Currently, he is living in Albuquerque, writing a novel, a collection of short stories entitled FIGHTIN', and editing an anthology of Native American Writing.

My Father's Song

Wanting to say things,
I miss my father tonight.
His voice, the slight catch,
the depth from his thin chest,
the tremble of emotion
in something he has just said
to his son, his song:

> We planted corn one Spring at Acu—
> we planted several times
> but this one particular time
> I remember the soft damp sand
> in my hand.

> My father had stopped at one point
> to show me an overturned furrow;
> the plowshare had unearthed
> the burrow nest of a mouse
> in the soft moist sand.

> Very gently, he scooped tiny pink animals
> into the palm of his hand
> and told me to touch them.
> We took them to the edge
> of the field and put them in the shade
> of a sand moist clod.

> I remember the very softness
> of cool and warm sand and tiny alive mice
> and my father saying things.

A New Story

Several years ago
I was a patient at the VA hospital
in Ft. Lyons, Colorado.
I got a message to call this woman,
so I called her up.
She said to me,
"I'm looking for an Indian.
Are you an Indian."
"Yes, I said.
"Oh good," she said,
"I'll explain why I'm looking
for an Indian."
And she explained.
"Every year, we put on a parade

in town, a Frontier Day Parade.
It's exciting and important,
and we have a lot of participation."
"Yes," I said.
"Well," she said, "Our theme
is Frontier,
and we try to do it well.
In the past, we used to make up
papier-maché Indians,
but that was years ago.
"Yes," I said.
"And then more recently,
we had some people
who dressed up as Indians
to make it more authentic,
you understand, real people."
"Yes," I said.
"Well," she said,
"that didn't seem right,
but we had a problem.
There was a lack of Indians."
"Yes," I said.
"This year, we wanted to do it right.
We have look hard and high
for Indians but there didn't seem
to be any in this part of Colorado."
"Yes," I said.
"We want to make it real, you understand,
put a real Indian on a float,
not just a papier-maché dummy
or an Anglo dressed as an Indian
but a real Indian with feathers and paint.
Maybe even a medicine man."
"Yes," I said.
"And then we learned the VA hospital
had an Indian here.
We were so happy,"
she said, happily.
"Yes," I said,
"there are several of us here."
"Oh good," she said.

Well, last Spring
I got another message
at the college where I worked.
I called the woman.
She was so happy
that I returned her call.
And then she explained

that Sir Francis Drake,
the English pirate
(she didn't say that, I did)
was going to land on the coast
of California in June, again.
And then she said
she was looking for Indians ...
"No," I said. No.

From *From Sand Creek*

At the Salvation Army
a clerk
caught me
wandering
among old spoons
            and knives,
                sweaters and shoes.

I couldn't have stolen anything;
my life was stolen already.

In protest though,
I should have stolen.
My life. My life.

She caught me;
Carson caught Indians,
secured them with his lies.
Bound them with his belief.

After winter,
our own lives fled.

I reassured her
what she believed.
Bought a sweater.

And fled.

I should have stolen.
My life. My life.

Indian Guys at the Bar

My head is drawing closer to the bar again
when someone says,

"Damn, my wife just lost her job,
I don't know what to do."

"Sometimes I drink;
other times I think I'm just crazy."

"Hey, here comes Jim. God, he's ugly."

"That's okay, brother, sit down.
Chippewas are always like that."

"Yeah, Chippewas were made to be like that."

The words jerk through me;
they vibrate and wobble for a long time.

"If them Pueblos ever learn to work,
they'll be okay."

"It's a cultural trait with them,
climb cliffs and throw rocks,
too tired to work."

"I heard three Indian guys got stabbed
downtown outside the Winstins.
Someone was watching them from the Federal Building
from the sixth floor where the BIA is."

Silence is sometimes the still wind;
sometimes it is the emptiness.

"I went to see my parole officer;
he said to behave or we'll send you back to the res."

"Man, when I was about to get out,
I heard the guard yell, '0367 Griego,
get your red ass in gear, you're going home,'
I couldn't believe it; I just stood there and cried."

"I know. I know. Here, have another drink
of culture."

I don't know if my feet can make it;
my soul is where it has always been;
my heart is staggering somewhere in between.

Survival This Way

Survival, I know how this way.
This way, I know.
It rains.
Mountains and canyons and plants
grow.
We travelled this way,
gauged our distance by stories
and loved our children.
We taught them
to love their births.
We told ourselves over and over
again, "We shall survive
this way."

Ted D. Palmanteer

"We have come a full circle with our culture. What was old and primitive has returned with new meaning and pride. That is what I'm painting, a new feeling, a new step, a new dance to a new song; but done with that old family pride."

Ted D. Tomeo-Palmanteer / Colville Indian, was born June 28, 1943 in Omak, Washington. After attending several schools throughout the state of Washington, he graduated from high school at the Institute of American Indian Arts, in Santa Fe, New Mexico in 1963. He graduated in 1973 from Central Washington State College, with a B.A. in a double major, one in Fine Arts and the other in Native American Studies. He taught at the Yakima Valley O.I.C. for two years, then he moved to Santa Fe and has been teaching there for the last two years. His work has been shown nationally and internationally. He has received numerous awards, and has participated in special shows with leading contemporary Indian artists. Most recently his works were included in an exhibit at the Via Gambaro Studio/Gallery, in Washington, D.C. and in a special December show at the "Trails End Galley, In the Oak House, S.W. 1st & Oak, Portland, Oregon.

192

Pass it on grandson

Granpa,
    he was a warrior
    wounds and cuts
    were his way,
    He was gruff
    and did as
    he pleased.

He solemnly
    instructed me,
    "If ever anyone
    questions you
    about protection;
    this is what
    you say,
    'Some things
    are passed on
    by blood alone,
    where mine goes
    or comes from
    is no one's concern,
    but my own."
    Way back in 47
    just before
    he took his last
    ride, wrapped in death.

Years later
    in '73
I graduated
from C.W.S.C.,
Went a celebraten'
to Wapato Town,
    and Indian bars.
Drinking and dancing!
    Pan's Cigar.
    (place of ill repute)

I made a toast
    on our fresh bottle,
    "Here's to my mom
    and all those
    who are not here
    with us now,
    but once they
    called this place,
    Second—Home.

We laughed
(after a brief moment of silence)
    as I spilled a cap
    of wine
    on the butt burned
    liquor soaked rug.

The bottle went,
    "round the horn,"
    as we drank
    from the cold springs.
    (Annie Green Springs)

I was zipping
    along at fast clip,
    dancing with
    some chik-a-dee
    who was out
    for a par-tee

When up sidled
    this old lady.
I knew I was, (in the presence),
    about to get the lean on.
She burst into
    laughter,
acting shrewd and wise.
(like she had medicine)

(In her guffaw)
She says,
"Teddy, do you remember
that place where
the old folks stayed,
or, were you *too little*.

(Teddy, I thought? Why's she
addressing me as my grandfather?)

I said to her,
    "Of course,
    I remember.
We lived on a hill;
below,
there was a stream,
it bubbled out of the
ground,
down there
where the rattlesnakes
used to lay
by the trail,
in the shade."

(I felt a rush,
feathers rustled,
she was an owl.)

The old lady laughed,
"Yes, that's the place.
Remember—that big rock,
to the right
of the old house,
by the cellar?"

"Sure," I answered,
(thinking, what's an
owl, just a mouth full
of feathers, to a
timber wolf?)

She looked perplexed,
(just for an instant),
then,
(like out of the way,
 not inquiringly),
mentioned,
"Oh,
that rock always
interested me;
there was brush
all around it
and little quail
would hide there,
right under *that* ledge.
I often wondered,
why, in a place
so full of snakes,
why, didn't they
go near that rock?
I was up there
just last weekend,
looking around,
now, I think
I've found the answer,
Your medicine is there.

"Yes, (I said, not boasting.),
    I remember people
looking there,
I often wondered
what for?
But,
do you know
what granpa
said to me?

(a little over anxiously),
She said,
"What, what did
he say?"
(acting like life would return
to her limbs.)

(with some malice and importance)
I answered,
"He said to me,
we moved,
to another hill!"

(couldn't help myself)

A dark cloud
covered her face,
she turned
to glare
at my smiling face,
(more like a
wolfish, mocking grin)
and she understood.

I have the blood,
something
like a hint,
from an
Old Warrior.

Granma's words

"When you are
ill at ease in
heart,
take a walk.

Do anything
that has to
be done.
Walk,
it out.

Walk alone,
in the hills
in the mountains.

Be strong
in the heart,
nothing lasts
forever.

Ron Rogers

Of himself, Ronald Rogers has said, "Born Claremore, Oklahoma, 20 November 1948. Cherokee/German/English. Christianpagan. (We all are. Educated at the Institute of American Indian Arts in Santa Fe, New Mexico and the University of California at Los Angeles. Graduated University of California, Santa Cruz, in 1973."

Co-author of MAN SPIRIT, a collection of poems, essays, and stories (with illustrations by Ted Palmanteer), he was a 1977 Fellow with the Newberry Library's Center for the History of the American Indian researching a book on the Indian side of the American Revolution. Currently living in Albuquerque, he has taught English, Creative Writing, and Journalism at Pikuni Community School on the Blackfeet Indian Reservation in Browning, Montana and been an instructor in Title Iv Indian Education Programs in Albuquerque. From 1973-76 he was an Instructor in Literal Arts at the Institute of American Indian Arts. Winner of two First Awards, Short Story Division, in the Scottsdale National Indian Arts Competition, his poems and stories have been anthologized in THE WHISPERING WIND (Doubleday), THE AMERICAN INDIAN SPEAKS (South Dakota Review Press), LITERATURE SKILLS FOR INDIAN ADULTS (American Indian Curriculum Development Project), NOVA (Scott-Foresman), and THE REMEMBERED EARTH (University of New Mexico Press).

Black Mesa

When the bloated sun stands   upon Black Mesa
Spider Woman weaves tapestries of skulls
Of plutonium and lillies.
This is the sunrise, long awaited, when
Dew glints, icy blood, on mountain passes;
The dawn when   will be heard
Songs made of deer and sweating horses.
(The new initiates   are here;
Here with papers, pencils, cameras,
To learn ceremonies   of atoms and fire.)
Striped blankets, rounded, on sandy vastness,
Turning, unstoppable, the wheel of the sun;
The mechanism is old beyond knowing,
Its operation skilled   beyond learning
Here, at sunrise, perfect circle balancing
Sand and shadow, wind and silence,
Was made a list of those who will die:
Mother, sister, father,
Brother; sunlight shines   alike
On dewdrops and steel: Teach us
Mother, father, grandfather,
Ghost, the meaning of that
Bloated sun   upon Black mesa.

(Here is a list of the things of the end of the world:
Eagles and ravens   intersecting
Drums that stir, in Memory's new silence,
Steel and skulls   flowers and cable wire
Rocks   mesas   cactus   blood.)

Bear Dance

Both Cherokee and Samek saw you, and tell
Of autumn leaves, of their passing.

Wrapped in the musk of your flesh I dance
To the sighing of winter trees.

Since the animals came, bearing fire,
We have danced in the shadow of the Stone Man.

The Death of Old Joe Yazzie

1.

Old Joe Yazzie died after working
Ten years in the uranium mines. He died
With his bones aflame, and the winds cried,
They are coming. They will be here pretty soon,
For over there a black cloud looms
Above Four Corners.

2.

A sound of puzzled thunder rose
Over the mesa
Where an eagle rode the high currents turning
The serpent-dry courses of arroyos far below
Where wisps of sunlight danced their vapors tracing
The ages in the strata of the pale desert stone
And the winds   the crying winds
Were full of butterflies, many colored.

Elf Night

In Oklahoma an old man died, long ago,
And the Elders sat in the moonlight and saw,
Before the bereaved relatives came to loot the house,
Some of the Little People, glowing with magic,
Making off with the flour and beans.

Montana Remembered From Albuquerque; 1982

1.

When winter nights fall like eyelids closing
Birds seek the shelter of the hollow trees
In the mountains   and remember
That avalanches can, and do, occur
At the sound of a single human voice
And that tufts of snow   drop
From pine branches
At the mention   of certain names.

2.

(In the Browning jailhouse: Suicide.
In the Great Falls jailhouse: A hanging, also
Suicide.
In the Cut Bank jailhouse: Another,
So that now a question must exist
As to whom they serve   and why
And what they feel
When they see that little white burro yonder,
That albino,   that sacred being.)

Horses lower their heads and graze the frozen grasses
In cold as bitter as needles and urine. A highway runs
Across the prairie, black,   broken,   undulating
Toward the lonely place where, waiting,
The eyeless men,   the policemen,
Red lights turning,
Move their shaded heads to mirror
Jailhouse cement, cracked, chilly to touch,
Porcelain rusted in clots by urine,
The clang of metal bars   also reflecting
The wildflowers there, on the prairie, where lie
The ancient dead,   at rest.

3.

In the weight of snow on pine branches   a delicacy
Greater
Than a moth's wing, or a human heart.

Self portrait

Rokwaho

We are created from Light. In the mysterious ways and wisdom of the Creator .. a star was born .. burned .. and died. From its ashes was birthed a new star .. Phoenix .. our Eldest Brother the Sun. The life and death of that first star, Mother Sun, created the elements of manifestations .. moons .. planets .. water, and loons . . .

From time to time, beings manifest who are destined to mentor and redirect the scheme and evolutionary flow of Humankind. They are the servants and stewards of the Creator's Dream. They bring into the realm of people and Creation .. knowledge and morality. They infuse us with Truth. The Knowledge and power and morality (the Truth and Desire of our Creator) exists in this world. Christ, Buddha, Deganawida, gave us the Truth of the way we should evolve and conduct ourselves as human beings. They all came bearing The Light of our Creator.

Deganawida gave us the Knowledge and the Power to prevent our extinction. Humankind is yet a child and an adolescent, but we are nearing the end of the Carnal Phase of our evolution. We still possess many instincts from our animal origins (which were essential to our survival as just one species on a teeming world), which if left unchecked would result in our extinction.

My head ebbs and wells to the music of the life that I was born into. Streams and waves of music engulf my solitude .. eternally .. and pass on by. The music is sunlight dancing .. playing .. gleaning across a crystall morning pond. It is the hushing sway of a Great White Pine .. grown to the artful whims of wind .. gently .. slowly .. molding cell by cell .. branch by branch .. one east .. one south .. one west .. one north .. one up .. one down. Wind grown pines are wind weaved patterns of music .. everchanging .. no two are ever the same because wind is a restless rover (and incidently, a very fine artist).

My own body is a drum. The rhythm within my being holds together all the other music in the universe .. in harmony. It is the universal conviction of them who have attained The Light that harmony comes from within. I understand this paradox .. I believe it. Music is the drum and keening of being .. and dance .. its celebration. All Creation is ceaseless song .. dance .. celebration. Water wells and chuckles above a liquid nether realm .. beguiling .. reflecting starlight from the eyes within. Water is the music .. the magic .. that begets the sentinel cawing of guileful crow in a world surreal .. a place where one may evolve into a glinting star in the eye of a loon ..

Water sings, water is, alive, water is alive. Water is drums. Round dance is Sundance .. Moondance .. Women's dance .. it is a dance of celebration and Earthhood. The Water Drum echoes the throbing rhythm of life being .. it echoes thunder .. water .. the drumming magic of Creation. Water's Drum quenches an eternal thirst .. earth .. life .. death .. earth .. and round and round and round .. until .... only The Light remains. Again ...

Clickstone

under the night shade
by barn and wild apple
where the shadows fade
wit and whim do grapple
where monsters are made
by fear and rain cackle
there clicks stone on blade
in shade of barn apple

click .. click .. stone .. clickstone
click .. stone .. rumours thunder
stone .. click .. slaps rain thrown
stone .. worn rain round, under
click .. stone .. rains alone
chips stone in barn blurr

clickstone endures the rain
little man whicks sparks red
thunderman grain by grain
clicks stone into arrow heads

under the night shade
where the shadows fade

Owl

(for Peter Brett)

I hear them .. the crickets
as relieved as I ..
that glaring cinder
has at last spent
its scorching passage.

A few hours of wounded relief ..
from the crimes committed,
conscienceless,
beneath its burning stare
.. as if impelled
by some mad ambition ..
to endure,
vindictive,
under that hellish shining.

The dusk is their cradle
.. their squint
betrays their peril ..
still they seek not
the twilight
when misfortune betides
our passage
too near to these
mortal reminders ..
haunting .. beguiling
the otherwise
pointless perfection
of black eternity ..

It is a night passage
for We
who know this.

There. It is behind us
at last .. and the darkness
returns, as ever, dark.

It will not be hard to find
some restless furr,
late among the rushes ..
his tiny eyes darting
in fear of my cloak!
This black conspiracy is death
to him who courts its mystery.
Its hallucinous presence comes
on my wing,
everywhere at once and
.. only skirmished silence
behind ..
my transfixing shadow.

We strike as one
pleasuring in the fresh
rending furr ..

We are reconciled
to steward the twilight ..
careless odds & ends.
'The Air Lords of No Fool's Land!'
If furr ever learns
to outwit his Bane,
I shall be no more.
.. an equable exchange
if I do say so myself ..

I see him now!
Tisk tisk. Furr down there
bending his own rules ..

We strike as one!
pleasuring in the fresh
rending Furr.

Gotcha! Fair & square ..
.. nothing personal.
Actually, Furr?
if you have a sense of humour
this is about as personal
as it is possible to get!
Awww Furr, not even a chuckle?
you had it coming
and so did I ..

There was a vacuum between us,
you and I.
And you know how Creation
just abhorrs a vacuum.
Thup! Just vacuum holes
sucking one into the other.
We are but the boiling surface
between eternity
and the circumference
of this hole
we live on, and on, and on ..

I wasted not a drop
of your blood, Furr.
Now! WE will strike as One
and pleasure in the fresh
rending furr.

It is a night passage
for WE
who know this.

Twoborn

(... prelude)

... a lake loon paddles
rings in the morning mirror ...
solitary .. gleaning the last
private dream in the burning
mist .. too soon the daily vigil
to outwit the fox's jaws
begins ...

... a bead of morningstar bobs
and falls from his shining bill ...
the mirror eddys its echo(((((((((
.. magic to the pebbled rim ..
a star is beached at the lip
of the singing mound ...

... the muffled chanting .. silent
now in the predawn .. is a loon's
memory .. midnight was the moon dance
... and morning sleeps a tired Owl ...
the singing mound breathes
a mushroom cloud .. fresh and warm
from the opened womb ...
naked .. the morningstar is born(e) ...

Twoborn

I have become without desire ...
to move ... or untwine
the grass that binds me ...

How real He seems ...
this realm of liquid veils
cannot eclipse His vision ...

Mine own blood and water
have soaked down the unquenchable
depths of earth ... my bones
bleach into stalagmite stone
formations ... and blinking agates
stud my brittle contours ...

How tall he seems above
the Great White Pine
He so gently uprooted ...
I felt not a thread root snap ...

My blood trickles past trout gills ...
Etching moon dance talismans
beneath the bottom beds ...

He has gathered my weapons
and buried them with my robe
and bones beneath the roots of Pine ...

I am become without desires ...
A blinking agate rises
from root to Pine cone
and glitters next
in the Eagle's twice born eyes ...

amber the sky
eyelid of the morning
opens sleep filmed
burning eye rising
high, backdropping shadows
hard, arctic white
stone mountains cold

steam crawled island
shore to shore to sheet
ice, straddles mile
wide, amplifies the chill
rarifies the lungs

athó came while
i slept and carved his art
outside, on the glass

a mystery to me
why he etched a season

of ferns & flowers & butterflies

athó (ah-thoe): spirit of the winter

Photo by Eugene Prince

Wendy Rose

I am that part of Indian Country that is young and in the process, still, of becoming self-defined. I was born in Oakland, California, in 1948, daughter of a Hopi man and a Miwok mixed blood woman from the region of Yosemite Park in the Sierras. My appearance is ambiguous enough for the local children to scream "Chink!" at me yet have my students at the University of California tell me "But you don't look Indian!" So, from early childhood, I have viewed myself as an "urban breed" and fantasized that I was so clearly one thing or another that no one would ever get it wrong. In some kind of unconscious recognition of my "hybrid" status, I have always had an identification with the centaur (although neither my Indian nor White blood is to be confused with the bestiality of the horse). Like the centaur, I have always felt misunderstood and isolated—whether with Indians or with non-Indians. This is important because it has a great deal to do with my poetry. The poetry, too, is hybrid—like me, there are elements of Indian-ness, of English-ness, of mythology, and of horse-ness. I am learning to be patient, not easy when you grow up with the noise of cars and trucks whizzing past. I am learning to be as tolerant of Indians who misunderstand me, as I have tried to be with non-Indians who have misunderstood me. I am learning to be proud of my urban, mixed heritage just as the occupants of Indian Country have had to learn to regain pride in Native heritage. I have come to believe that I represent Indian Country as legitimately as any fullblood, as any person fluent in their Native language—not to be confused with representing Hopi or Miwok, or, for that matter, England. My poetry is the tool I have used to come to terms with this—not only my poetry, really, but the poetry of other occupants of this section of Indian Country. I am thankful that I am now old enough to take great joy in "discovering" young talent and am beginning to "collect" young Indian poets as I was once "collected". So, a special hello and welcome to the neighborhood for Linda Noel, Lance Horseman, Pam Green and Janice Gould! And a wink to Joe Bruchac for giving me the opportunity to return everything ten years after he published my very first book.

Straight gig: full-time faculty at University of California, Berkeley, in Native American Studies/Ethnic Studies, 1979-present. Part-time faculty in Anthropology (!?), Contra Costa College, San Pablo, CA, 1982-present.

Books published: Hopi Roadrunner Dancing (Greenfield Review Press, 1973); Long Division: A Tribal History (Strawberry Press, 1976. Reprinted 1981-2); Academic Squaw: Reports to the World from the Ivory Tower (Blue Cloud Press, 1977); Poetry of the American Indian Series: Wendy Rose (American Visual Communications Bank, 1978—multi media); Builder Kachina: A Home-going Cycle (Blue Cloud Press, 1979); Aboriginal Tattooing in California (University of California Archaeological Research Facility, 1979—not poetry); Lost Copper (Malki Museum Press, Morongo Indian Reservation, 1980); What Happened When the Hopi Hit New York (Contact II Publications, 1982); The Man Who Dreamed He Was Turquoise (with Roy Albert, in progress—bilingual Hopi-English); Dancing For the Whiteman (in progress); The Halfbreed Chronicles & Other Poems (in progress); Letters Home: Neon Scars (in progress). Also included in about 40 anthologies and about 50 journals.

The well-intentioned question

Here you are
asking me again
what is my Indian name

and this was the time
I promised myself
I'd tell the truth

and stand hard
and smooth
as madrone,

tight as mesquite
answering you.
My Indian name soars

in pinyon-wood flutes,
stopped at one end
by asphalt; my Indian name

catapults
like condors gliding inland
on the power of prayer;

my Indian name bumps
on the backs
of obsidian-hard women

sighting me with eyes
Coyote gave them;
my Indian name howls

around the black hats
of fullblood men
on Friday-night search

for fairness or failing that
for fullness;
my Indian name listens

for footsteps
stopping short of my door
then leaving forever.

208

Sarah: Cherokee Doctor

Her touch heals
in the great sip
of prairie wind
over ancient plains
gusting
        a power
        mountain born
        a song   ochre grass
        held like needles
        on the tongue
        and blown
        into radiance.
One year she
was that woman
kneeling on the edge of camp.
You could see her there.
Sun Dancers spun before her,
vision-tracking warriors
pledged to spin
til the songs were done
and the flesh was torn.
Her healing hands
fragrant
with the scratch of sweet-grass
the whisper of dew
sends them away as they come
her many sons
weeping to her breast.   They slept
she said, shivering against her
in their sweat.
And she touched their dripping hair
and steady restored them
to lock deep the memory
in their flutes,
give their eyes up
to incessant sun,
bone to the earth
and balance
to each day done
turn by turn
sweat by sweat
prayer by prayer
dropping about the pole
like human heart's blood
or the tears of an eagle.

Now she is kneeling again
at the lectern
in the boardroom,
warriors resting yet

at her breast.
Her voice is singing
through university halls
that high clear sound
that incantation
we have come to know.
She struggles
to keep us well mannered and fat,
bearing us like her unborn children
and we keep her magic
memorized.
The journey must be
away from her
as tiny fish dart
from the strength of their mother.
We will be healed
in the shadow
of her dancing shawl
covering fringe
inch by inch
feet first then hip
to shoulder and mouth
the lover
whose brown arms
twist about us
and keep the amulets
intact.

Julia

[*Julia Pastrana, 1832-1860, was a singer and dancer billed in the circus as
"Lion Lady" or "The World's Ugliest Woman". She was a Mexican Indian born
with facial deformities and silky hair growing from everywhere on her body. In
an effort to maintain control over her professional life, her manager persuaded
her that he wanted to marry her. Believing he was sincere, they were married
and some months later she bore a son. The child looked exactly like her and
lived for only six hours after birth. A few days later, Julia also died. Her
manager-husband, still unwilling to lose control, had Julia Pastrana and her
infant boy preserved and mounted in an upright cabinet of wood and glass. As
recently as 1975, Julia and her baby were exhibited at locations in the United
States and in Europe. Their current location is unknown*]

Tell me it was just a dream,
my husband, a clever trick
made by some tin-faced village god
or ghost-coyote pretending to frighten me
with his claim that our marriage
is made of malice and money.
Oh tell me again how you admire my hands,

how my jasmine tea is rich and strong,
my singing sweet, my eyes so dark
you would lose yourself swimming
man into fish
as you mapped the pond
you would own.
That was not all.
The room grew cold
as if to joke with these warm days;
the curtains blew out
and fell back against
the moon-painted sill.
I rose from my bed like a spirit
and, not a spirit at all,
floated slowly
to my great glass oval
to see myself reflected
as the burnished bronze woman,
skin smooth and tender,
I know myself to be in the dark
above the confusion
of French perfumes
and I was there in the mirror
and I was not.
I had become hard
as the temple stones of Otomi,
hair grown over my ancient face
like black moss, gray as jungle fog
soaking green the tallest tree tops.
I was frail
as the breaking dry branches
of my winter sand canyons
standing so still
as if to stand
forever.
Oh such a small room!
No bigger than my elbows outstretched
and just as tall as my head.
A small room
from which to sing open the doors
with my cold graceful mouth,
my rigid lips, my silences
dead as yesterday, cruel as the children,
and cold as the coins
that glitter in your pink fist.
And another magic
in the cold of that smallest of rooms—
in my arms or standing near me
on a tall table by my right side
a tiny doll
that looked
like me ...

Oh my husband, tell me again
this is only a dream
I wake from warm
and today is still today,
summer sun and quick rain;
tell me, husband, how you love me
for my self one more time.
It scares me so
to be with child,
lioness
with cub.

Otomi: site of Indian ruins in Mexico

How I came to be a graduate student

It was when my songs became quiet.
No one was threatened,
no eyes kept locked on my red hands
to see if they would steal
the beads and silver from museum shelves.
When I became, in the owl's way, a hunter
they trusted the microscope
that hid me in the grass, that bent up
and over me too big to drive away.
That's how they knew
they could move in.

Those quiet songs
I could tell you
simply expose the stone spirit
of Warrior Kachina stepping sideways
through the village; or I could say
that the brave and ragged meat of me
is being tongued away by a foreign god.
I am shut away in a house
where all are dead and when it looks
like I may break loose they tell me
I'm *moving* now and congratulations ...
all the time my stone-spirit song
grows and erupts and laps over the world;
my legs roll away like water on stone
going downhill to an ancient matrix,
uprooting in the spring and moving on.
It's that kind of moving:
from grave to grave.

Loo-wit

The way they do
this old woman
no longer cares what
others think
but spits her black tobacco
any which way she wants
stretching full length
on her bumpy bed.
Finally up she sprinkles
ash on the snow,
cold and rocky ribs
promising nothing
but that winter is gone.
Centuries of berries
have bound her to earth.
Her children play games
(no sense of tomorrow);
her eyes covered with bark
she wakes at night
and fears she is blind.
Nothing but tricks
left in this world;
nothing to keep
an old woman home.
Around her machinery growls,
snarls and ploughs
great patches
of green grey skin.
She crouches in the north,
the source of the trembling dawn
with the shudder
of her slopes.
Blackberries unravel,
stones dislodge;
it's not as if they weren't warned.

She was sleeping
but she heard the boot scrape,
the creaking floor,
felt the pull of the blanket
from her thin shoulder.
With one free hand
she finds her weapons
and raises them high,
clearing the twigs from her throat
she sings, she sings,
trembling all of the sky about her
Loo-wit sings and sings and sings.

Loo-wit: Mount Saint Helens

Photo by Paul Shuttleworth

Norman H. Russell

Born Nov 28, 1921, Big Stone Gap, Virginia. College at Slippery Rock State Teachers, Pa. (B.S.), and University of Minnesota (Ph.D. in Botany), in 1951.

Have taught at Grinnell College, Buena Vista College, Rutgers University, Arizona State University, and now at Central State Universtiy, Edmond, Okla.

Publications: 13 books and workbooks in Botany, 15 books and chapbooks of poetry. Many scientific and literary magazine publications.

Heritage ⅛ Cherokee Indian.

With my poems I have particularly attempted to recreate the lives of pre-columbian peoples on Turtle Island.

The Cherokee Dean

they are not automobiles
they are horses
and that is not a condominium
it is a cliff of stone houses
the janitor brings the mail
he is a runner from a distant village
i had to fire a professor
now he must stand in the shadows
he cannot come to the circle in the night
it is cold outside the furnace is laboring
i send a young man to look for sticks
we go to the refrigerator for a snack
there is nothing not even a track
the deer have formed their snow circle
two hills beyond.

The Tree Sleeps in the Winter

the tree sleeps in the winter he
moves where the wind wishes him he
returns and he nods his head like
the child in the afternoon but he
cannot lie down

does the tree think thoughts
in the winter does he remember
the summer does he stand in
the snow waiting can the tree wait
as i wait?

do the trees speak down mountains do
they call shouts from the top snow
coming from the bottom saying the bear
sleeps do the trees listen
to each other?

does the tree sleeping feel the bird
scratching and scratching the squirrel
pushing his sleepy back the deer
rubbing his soft horn the sun
speaking saying come awake it is spring now?

Appearance

as the tree does not end
at the tip of its root or branch
as the bird does not end
with its feathers or flight
as the earth does not end
with its tallest mountain

so also i do not end
with my arm my foot my skin
but continue reaching outward
into all of space and all of time
with my voice and my thoughts
for my soul is the universe

though you see the bird here
he is also there
the bird the tree and you and i
are only here because your eye
and your mind has put us here
we are as wind that may not be held.

The Tornado

just when he said the tornado
is now located at and moving at miles per hour
the television set went black
black as the sky black as death
black as the hell outside
black as the closet we groped into
falling all down with blankets and dresses
clutching each other our hearts pounding
loud as the pounding of the wind on the windows
gasping for breath holding our breath
like the wind outside roaring and pausing
then the great chunking of the short thunder
imprisoned in the small black animal
of a cloud rushing among the oak trees
went on east we heard it go we heard it talking
to the people in the eastern houses
and we sat still holding each other
still a long time yet in the black closet
slow to come back from the black
from the death in the teeth of the tornado.

The Message of the Rain

when i was a child
i was a squirrel a bluejay a fox
and spoke with them in their tongues
climbed their trees dug their dens
and knew the taste
of every grass and stone
the meaning of the sun
the message of the night

now i am old and past
both work and battle
and know no shame
to go alone into the forset
to speak again to squirrel fox and bird
to taste the world
to find the meaning of the wind
the message of the rain.

Ralph Salisbury

Ralph Salisbury's Cherokee people were spared the Death March to Oklahoma, their escape secured by the martyrdom of Tsali and his sons. Life, until he turned 18 and went into the Air Force, was about as close to the old days as possible—hunting, planting, and finding spirit-awareness in Nature—even though he grew up in Iowa, far from the old ground.

His father had only two years of school and was a traditional story-teller and, also, a singer, self taught on five-string banjo, which he carved with his pocket knife from a hickory limb and a wooden cigar box. Victims of repressive economic policies, the family lived at near starvation level through several winters, losing one child. America's World War Two prosperity improved their lot. For his military service, Ralph Salisbury received six years of university education, studying with writers James Hearst, Robie Macauley, R. V. Cassill, Paul Engle and Robert Lowell.

He has worked as a farm laborer, construction worker, janitor, photographer, journalist, university professor, literary editor, fiction writer and poet. Of his poems and fiction, he says, "I try to speak for people who have to struggle hard for any sense of dignity, well-being and beauty in their lives. I am one of them."

His poems and stories have appeared in many magazines and anthologies in English, Canada and The U.S. including CHARITON REVIEW, GREENFIELD REVIEW, POETRY, NEW YORKER, NORTHWEST REVIEW, SPAWNING THE MEDICINE RIVER, TRANSATLANTIC REVIEW, MASSACHUSETTS REVIEW, and CONTEMPORARY POETS OF THE WESTERN UNITED STATES.

His books are GHOST GRAPEFRUIT AND OTHER POETS from Ithaca House, POINTING AT THE RAINBOW from Blue Cloud Press, SPIRIT BEAST

CHANT *from Blue Cloud Press and* GOING TO THE WATER: POEMS OF A
CHEROKEE HERITAGE *from Pacific House Books.*

For five years he was editor of NORTHWEST REVIEW. *He is editor of an
anthology of contemporary Native American writing* THE NATION WITHIN,
from Outrigger Publishers, New Zealand.

*He is Professor of English at the University of Oregon in Eugene, where he
lives with his wife, poet Ingrid Wendt, and their daughter. In 1983, he will be
Fulbright Professor in Native American Literature at J W Goethe University,
Frankfurt, W. Germany.*

By Now

"Feet just like ice" say
my Cherokee grandmother's stories
of children lost in the woods, woods lost,

long since, to White men's money-making blades,
to termites ticking like time-bombs and
to forgetting's woodpecker-beak.

What were they like? those maples, whose,
few, descendants I bled, in my
childhood, in spring, for syrup and sugar, for Grandma,
my augur like remembering
or prayer tapping growth-rings'
sweeter and sweeter seasons—

what were they like?
to be lost in
midst wolves and awesome ancestor-bears and the sky

leaves dark as eclipse planets clustered
as thick as bats,
and, in black dirt, which a glacier had spaded,
my toes—
icicle roots
I know, by now, must melt.

Three Migrations

(for my son, Brian, on his birthday, 14 July, Bastille Day, 1982)

I

The year our neighbors' ancestors' Thor
or our Cherokee God of Rain sent sun-
fish, northern pike, bass and carp
to graze
in our pasture,
Teacher sermonized that The Ordovician
Period had come again,
and I wrote it "fish'n".

II

"Trash-fish" in bank-loan-waiting-room
Field and Stream—

weeks without meat, we were able to afford:
sheepshead, quillback, squawfish and carp

out of ice off the back of a truck moving slow
as a glacier through drouth

and gratefully ate—
                    "trout"
gleaming like the bumpers
of the banker's latest car.

III

When The Mississippi, which
Cherokees crossed mid-winter—
Death March to Oklahoma—flooded,
spring-thaw, and invaded our pasture,

where it had once been
right at home, with dinosaurs
crawling like fleas through its rippling fur,

sixteen and almost ready to join the army
and save democracy and earn an education,

I waded to bring home
our dairy herd,

my untrimmed toes
schools of minnows,
scales on their heads
blunt compass needles, I follow,
three wars later, as well as I can.

This Is My Death-Dream

I'm three I'm balancing
the family barn
on my thumb
and I'm thickening inside
even my brain
even my thoughts
thickening

this is the doctor
who has done all medicine can
and my fever will either break or I'll die

this is my father
an ice storm of tears on the Chevrolet windshield
to town for ice cream
though the late night roads are drifted almost closed
though there is not enough money
he makes that hard journey but
I am unconscious and can not eat
let him leave ice cream on my grave till spring
wilts it let my gratitude bloom on his
though in under a year drunk again
he'll shoot a demon's circle around my feet
old wood splintered new white
the kitchen floor
shaking under my toes
splinters thrust up like the thorns of a crown
in the picture above the hallway mirror

this is my memory
barn teetering huge on the earth that is always
a crescent moon black
beneath the nail of my thumb
the animals terrified
how can they believe that a three year old
will not drop them to smash amid kindling
how can they know that lightning
that fever of the heavens
will burn the barn before I am into my teens
and the only way
they are going to be saved
is for me to survive being struck
by lightning just before I go to war
bolt hitting fence built to keep livestock
from oats they like as much as I like ice cream
and for me to remember them

this is the thickening
it's maybe as if all the growth of my life span
is crowding like loved ones into a poem or citizens fleeing
a city about to be bombed

by the B-24's I'll fly in for 26 months 300 hours
see 90 crewmen die and 27 years later still feel
myself in one
plane called "flying barn" teetering on an invisible thumb

"Among the Savages . . ."

Atop its mound frosted white
as the dome of *Sacre Coeur*—

cathedral on a hill in Paris—

ripe corn—golden-hosted, many-armed Indian-
brown crucifix—takes
communion-wine dawn

and begins a memorial-
service for the French Jesuit, Father Priber,

his Cherokee dictionary, five years of devoted work
"among the savages . . . lost"—

and his life—

in English Colonial prison,
which he'd earlier saved from burning—

a century before Sequoia

did it all again,
lived to do it twice,
his first syllabary—
berry-juice on birch-bark—
torched by his soon-to-be ex-
wife angry at his wasting his time—

The Anglican Church and Rome
fighting like dogs over bones
dancing, in Earth
around the sun, thanks
for the gift of corn.

A Second Molting

"War-bonnet" we'd say,
chicken-yard plucked,
a second molting,
and hawks' wings rose
from brows of Dad's "Best Shots", but,

above black head-bands scalped from innertube
miles stabbed
by nail rust put
to ritual fire, white eagle-plumed bombers shamed—
    with newspaper-facts in rows
    straighter than blue-jacket troops'—the worst
stories we
war-bonneted braves ever had
heard.

Leslie Silko

Leslie Marmon Silko was born in Albuquerque, New Mexico in 1948. Of mixed ancestry—Laguna Pueblo, Mexican, and white—she grew up on the Laguna Pueblo Reservation. A graduate of the University of New Mexico, where she also studied for three semesters in the American Indian Law Program before deciding to devote herself fulltime to writing, she has taught at the University of New Mexico and the University of Arizona. Widely anthologized, both as a poet and a short story writer, she is included in Best Short Stories of 1975, Two Hundred Years of Great American Short Stories, Carriers of the Dream Wheel *and* The Remembered Earth. *Most recently she had been deeply involved in film-making with her Laguna Film Project and she is working on a new novel which she hopes to complete in 1984. Her achievement as a writer has been recognized by a National Endowment for the Arts Writing Fellowship and a MacArthur Foundation award. Her books include LAGUNA WOMAN, a collection of poetry (Greenfield Review Press); CEREMONY, a novel; and STORYTELLER, a book which "re-creates the ancient stories in prose and poetry (the distinction for the Native American is far less than in the European tradition), spicing them with the realities of her own experience."*

223

Where Mountainlion Laid Down With Deer
February, 1973

I climb the black rock mountain
    stepping from day to day
                silently.
I smell the wind for my ancestors
      pale blue leaves
      crushed wild mountain smell.
Returning
      up the grey stone cliff
      where I descended
            a thousand years ago.
Returning to faded black stone
       where mountainlion laid down with deer.

It is better to stay up here
       watching wind's reflection
      in tall yellow flowers.
The old ones who remember me are gone
     the old songs are all forgotten
     and the story of my birth.

     How I danced in snow-frost moonlight
       distant stars to the end of the Earth,
     How I swam away
       in freezing mountain water
       narrow mossy canyon tumbling down
           out of the mountain
           out of deep canyon stone
     down
       the memory
           spilling out
           into the world.

Story from Bear Country

You will know
when you walk
in bear country
By the silence
flowing swiftly between the juniper trees
by the sundown colors of sandrock
all around you.

You may smell damp earth
scratched away
from yucca roots
You may hear snorts and growls
slow and massive sounds
from caves
in the cliffs high above you.

It is difficult to explain
how they call you
All but a few who went to them
left behind families
        grandparents'
        and sons
        a good life.

The problem is
you will never want to return

Their beauty will overcome your memory
like winter sun
melting ice shadows from snow
And you will remain with them
locked forever inside yourself
        your eyes will see you
        dark shaggy and thick.

We can send bear priests
loping after you
their medicine bags
bounding against their chests
Naked legs painted black
bear claw necklaces
rattling against
their capes of blue spruce.

They will follow your trail
into the narrow canyon
through the blue-gray mountain sage
to the clearing
where you stopped to look back
and saw only bear tracks
behind you.

When they call
faint memories
will writhe around your heart
and startle you with their distance.
But the others will listen
because bear priests sing
beautiful songs
they must
if they are ever to call you back.

They will try to bring you
step by step
back to the place you stopped
and found only bear prints in the sand
where your feet had been.

Whose voice is this?
You may wonder
hearing this story when
after all
you are alone
hiking in these canyons and hills
while your wife and sons are waiting
back at the car for you.

But you have been listening to me
for some time now
from the very beginning in fact
and you are alone in this canyon of stillness
not even cedar birds flutter.

See, the sun is going down now
the sandrock is washed in its colors
Don't be afraid
    we love you
    we've been calling you
    all this time

Go ahead
turn around
see the shape
of your footprints
in the sand.

     He was a small child
     learning to get around
      by himself.
     His family went by wagon
     into the mountains near
      Fluted Rock.

     It was Fall and
     they were picking piñons.
     I guess he just wandered away
    trying to follow his brothers and sisters
      into the trees.

His aunt thought he was with his mother,
and she thought he was with his sister.

When they tracked him the next day
his tracks went into the canyon
near the place which belonged
to the bears. They went
as far as they could
to the place
where no human
could go beyond,
and his little footprints
were mixed in with bear tracks.

So they sent word for this medicine man
to come. He knew how
to call the child back again.

There wasn't much time.
The medicine man was running, and his
assistants followed behind him.

They all wore bearweed
tied at their wrists and ankles
and around their necks.

He grunted loudly and scratched on the ground in front of him
he kept watching the entrance of the bear cave.

He grunted and made a low growling sound.
Pretty soon the little bears came out
because he was making mother bear sounds.
He grunted and growled a little more
and then the child came out.
He was already walking like his sisters
he was already crawling on the ground.

The couldn't just grab the child.
They couldn't simply take him back
because he would be in-between forever
and probably he would die.

They had to call him.
Step by step the medicine man
brought the child back.

So, long time ago
they got him back again
but he wasn't quite the same
after that
not like the other children.

Toe'osh: A Laguna Coyote Story

for Simon Ortiz, July, 1973

1

In the wintertime
at night
we tell coyote stories
          and drink Spanada by the stove.
How coyote got his
ratty old fur coat
        bits of old fur
        the sparrows stuck on him
        with dabs of pitch.
That was after he lost his proud original one in a poker game.
anyhow, things like that
are always happening to him,
that's what she said, anyway.

And it happened to him at Laguna
and Chinle
and at Lukachukai too, because coyote got too smart for his own good.

2

But the Navajos say he won a contest once.
It was to see who could sleep out in a
snow storm the longest
and coyote waited until chipmunk badger and skunk were all
curled up under the snow
and then he uncovered himself and slept all night
inside
and before morning he got up and went out again
and waited until the others got up before he came
in to take the prize.

3

Some white men came to Acoma and Laguna a hundred years ago
and they fought over Acoma land and Laguna women, and even now
some of their descendants are howling in
the hills southeast of Laguna.

4

Charlie Coyote wanted to be governor
and he said that when he got elected
he would run the other men off
the reservation
and keep all the women for himself.

5

One year
the politicians got fancy
at Laguna.
They went door to door with hams and turkeys
and they gave them to anyone who promised
to vote for them.
On election day all the people
stayed home and ate turkey
and laughed.

6

The Trans-Western pipeline vice president came
to discuss right-of-way.
The Lagunas let him wait all day long
because he is a busy and important man.
And late in the afternoon they told him
to come back again tomorrow.

7

They were after the picnic food
that the special dancers left
down below the cliff.
And Toe'osh and his cousins hung themselves
down over the cliff
holding each other's tail in their mouth making a coyote chain
until someone in the middle farted
and the guy behind him opened his
mouth to say "What stinks?" and they
all went tumbling down, like that.

8

Howling and roaring
Toe'osh scattered white people
out of bars all over Wisconsin.
He bumped into them at the door
until they said
               'Excuse me'
And the way Simon meant it
was for 300 or maybe 400 years.

R. T. Smith

I was born in Washington, D.C. but raised in Georgia and North Carolina, where I received my education at the University and at Appalachian State University (M.A.). My family background is Scotch-Irish and Tuscarora.

I am presently Poet-in-residence at Auburn University in Alabama, where I teach composition, world lit, poetry writing and southern lit.

My main interest as a poet involves a low threshold of attention, the way the world patterns itself in small ways to suggest the great circle of life. This happens in language, as well as in the ways the world celebrates itself in visual rituals. Most importantly, though, what interests me as a poet is what interests me as a man.

Publications: Waking Under Snow, Cold Mountain Press, 1975; Good Water, *Tamarack Editions, 1979;* Rural Route, *Tamarack Editions, 1981;* Beasts Did Leap, *Tamarack Editions, 1982;* From the High Dive, *Water Mark Press, 1983;* Finding The Path, *Black Willow, 1983.*

Yonosa House

She stroked molten tones
from the heart-carved maple dulcimer.
My grandma did.
She sat like a noble sack of bones
withered within coarse skin,
rocking to snake or corn tunes,
music of passing seasons.
She sang the old songs.

Her old woman's Tuscarora uncut hair
hung like waxed flax ready to spin
till she wove it to night braids,
and two tight-knotted ropes
lay like lanyards on her shoulders.
On my young mind she wove
the myths of the race
in fevered patterns, feathery colors:
Sound of snow, kiss of rock,
the feel of bruised birch bark,
the call of the circling hawk.

Her knotted hands showing slow blue rivers
jerked nervously through cornbread frying,
pressed fern patterns on butter pats,
brewed sassafras tea in the hearth.
She wore her lore and old age home.

They buried Yonosa in a doeskin skirt,
beads and braids, but featherless,
like a small bird with clipped wings.
I cut hearts on her coffin lid,
wind-slain maple like the dulcimer.
The mountain was holy enough for Yonosa.
We kept our promise and raised no stone.
She sank like a root to be red Georgia clay.
No Baptist churchyard caught her bones.

I thank her hands when the maple leaves turn,
hear her chants in the thrush's song.

Red Anger

The reservation school is brown and bleak
with bugs' guts mashed against walls
and rodent pellets reeking in corners.
Years of lies fade into the black chalk board.
A thin American flag with 48 stars
hangs lank over broken desks.
The stink of stale piss haunts the halls.

Tuscarora.

My reservation home is dusty.
My mother grows puffy with disease,
her left eye infected open forever.
Outside the bedroom window
my dirty, snotty brother Roy
claws the ground,
scratching like the goat who gnaws the garden.

Choctaw.

My father drinks
pale moonshine whiskey
and gambles recklessly at the garage,
kicks dust between weeds in the evening
and dances a fake-feathered rain dance
for tourists and a little cash.
Even the snakes have left.
Even the sun cannot stand to watch.

Cherokee.

Our limping dog sniffs a coil of hot shit
near the outhouse where
my sister shot herself with a .22.
So each day I march
two miles by meagre fields
to work in a tourist lunch stand
in their greasy aprons.
I nurse my anger like a seed,
and the whites would wonder why
I spit in their hamburgers.

Tuscarora, Choctaw, Cherokee. . .
the trail of tears never ends.

The Long Joke

The Plains Indians had a game
in which one tribe imitated another,
mimed their dress, medicine bags,
parfleche and paint. A stranger
coming into camp might mistake
Crow for Cheyenne, Paiute for Sioux,
and never know he had been fooled.
In the Winter of the White Buffalo
a Dakota brave entered a hunting camp
on the Lower Rosebud, convinced
he was meeting friendly Oglala.
Three days he stayed, took pemmican
and slept in one clan's lodge,
warmed his heart by their fire and tales.
When he left, gifts changed hands—
a steel-headed axe, a wampum band,
plumes from a blue bird with no name.
A year later the brave discovered
he had stayed with his sworn enemy,
the nomad Arapaho. He believed he could
hear the grass laughing. In rage he
searched the Black Hills, called
on every Manitou he knew for revenge.
But the Long Joke tribe was gone,
vanished into the river, risen
into clouds or dissolved in pollen.
In dust he tore his hair and swore
to live alone forever, so great
a fool did he feel. But what he
suffered seems to miss the point.
The false band became a legend, lost
in Canada's snow. They played the Long
Joke for fifteen years, forgot the sound
of their native tongue and dream,
became their own final victims.

And so it seems some sadness cannot die.
Today when you look around, the old
Long Joke is being played by every
surviving tribe, dancing to no music,
following the bird with no name.

Beneath the Mound

Deer, lightning, bluebird, toad—
someone has drawn figures
on the small walls of my chamber,
this hollow under a hill.
I can hear the thirsty roots stretching.
I can feel the damp soil settling.
I sleep uneasily and long to be whole.

Most of my weapons, masks and tools
are dust. Most of my vessels
are broken, returned to their source.
The cloth that once wrapped me
has lost all holding power.
My bones are strewn out
and cannot be healed.
Dark stones in a pattern
are the only stars I behold.

Who remembers that night,
that fire, the weeping women
and a procession, slaves hauling
earth to build this mound?
Who recalls the sacred chants?
Who can dance the steps of death?
Who knows the dialect
and stories that identified my tribe?

If I could weave my spirit to memory,
my memory to ligament and muscle,
I could gather these fragments,
scattered and anxious to be found.
If I could recover the taste
of the black yaupon drink or skills
that kept my hunting silent,
I could refledge this dusty flesh.
I could quench this urge to move.

But history holds me in its grip,
an owl with his captive rat
moving deeper into night,
a rock preventing the spring's water
from surfacing under the moon.
If I could get this cracked jaw to move,
I could rise to summon the rain.
If I could see the sky at all,
I would catch the bluebird by his wing.
If I could speak,
I would sing.

Photo by B. U. Zuckerman (1977)

Mary TallMountain

I was born Mary Demonski in the Interior of Alaska. My folks were Athabaskan-Russian and Scotch-Irish. I was adopted at three when Mom became consumptive in 1921. The doctor and his wife who brought me up in Unalaska and Dillingham, tutored me at home because the schools were so poor in the territory then.

I was a legal secretary in San Francisco from 1945, and began publishing in literary journals around 1960, then after Paula Gunn Allen tutored me in fiction for two years, I started a novel set in Nulato, on the Yukon River where I was born. It's called DOYON, the Indian name for Chief or Wolverine. I may title it There is No Word for Goodbye, too, same title as my little book of poems. The novel is ²/₃ done.

I began using the name Tall Mountain, because I did a lot of climbing of small mountains early on, and always loved that kind of country because of my first memories of the far Kaiyuh Mts.

I retired and now have re-entered the financial world, learning to do word processing. I found the entry fascinating from a writer's viewpoint, and my own 64-year old stance. I work with lots of young people and am compiling lots of character sketches and every day's filled with material for my IBM. I really enjoy getting this new knowledge of the technological society. It is a strange and marvelous world, and the people who inhabit it are, like me, strange and wonderful and magic.

Good Grease

The hunters went out with guns
at dawn.
We had no meat in the village,
no food for the tribe and the dogs.
No caribou in the caches.

All day we waited.
At last!
As darkness hung at the river
we children saw them far away.
Yes! They were carrying caribou!
We jumped and shouted!

By the fires that night
we feasted.
The old ones clucked,
sucking and smacking,
sopping the juices with sourdough bread.
The grease would warm us
when hungry winter howled.

Grease was beautiful,
oozing,
dripping and running down our chins,
brown hands shining with grease.
We talk of it
when we see each other
far from home.

Remember the marrow
sweet in the bones?
We grabbed for them like candy.
Good.
Gooooood.

Good grease.

Indian Blood

On the stage I stumbled,
my fur boot caught
on a slivered board.
Rustle of stealthy giggles.

Beendaaga' made of velvet
crusted with crystal beads
hung from brilliant tassels of wool,
wet with my sweat.

Children's faces stared.
I felt their flowing force.
Did I crough like *goh*
in the curious quiet?

They butted to the stage,
darting questions; pointing.
Do you live in an igloo?
Hah! You eat blubber!

Hemmed in by ringlets of brass,
grass-pale eyes,
the fur of *daghooda-aak*
trembled.

Late in the night
I bit my hand until it was
pierced
with moons of dark
Indian blood.

beendaaga'	mittens
goh	rabbit
daghooda-aak	caribou parka

There Is No Word for Goodbye

Sokoya, I said, looking through
        the net of wrinkles into
        wise black pools
        of her eyes.

What do you say in Athabaskan
        when you leave each other?
        What is the word
        for goodbye?

A shade of feeling rippled
        the wind-tanned skin.
        Ah, nothing, she said,
        watching the river flash.

She looked at me close.
        We just say, Tłaa. That means,
        See you.
        We never leave each other.
        When does your mouth
        say goodbye to your heart?

She touched me light
        as a bluebell.
        You forget when you leave us;
        you're so small then.
        We don't use that word.

We always think you're coming back,
        but if you don't,
        we'll see you some place else.
        You understand.
        There is no word for goodbye.

           Sokoya: Aunt (mother's sister)

Ts'eekkaayah

In the month of Beaver
I watch the night sky,
Thinking this was the time of year
We made *ts'eekkaayah*.
Memories stretch and pull around me—
Bark drying on a new canoe.

Hunters sprawl by the fire,
Outcamp bread bubbles in grease,
Duck soup gurgles
In the old black dutch oven.
'Way off, drifting through *kk'eeyh*
Fat smells drown our mouths.

Mom calls, *"Onee!"*
Yelling we race to camp,
Tumbling brown bear cubs.
Uncle and Papa grumble at us
In gruff voices
I have heard for a lifetime.

Listen. My brothers are singing.
Bernie squeaks a high note,
Makes Billy start giggling.
They wrestle awhile.
After supper they make caribou song,
Honking on a tin harmonica.

Echoing cloud voices call
Over Nulato, over *Kkaayah*,
High over Denali, over Chugach,
Over miles of islands,
Years of dancing, mourning,
Loving, dying.

Crowfeather shadows crawl
Along thin blue edges of *tsaghał.*
Great horned owl sails low,
Winter-grey wings fan the river,
Her yellow eyes blazing
Threaten bad luck *yeega'.*

We yawn into our beds
Inside a ring of sleeping dogs.
Papa says they keep away *nak'aghon.*
We snug down furry,
Billy and me, wrapped in
Dark music of spruce trees.

Miyeets flows through our spirits
From forest, flames, owl's wings.
Our breath is one
Under the high shining eye
Of *Dołtol*
Walking through the sky.

ts'eekkaayah	spring camp or home
kk'eeyh	birches
Onee!	Come here!
Kkaayah	ancient Kaiyuh country
Denali	Mt. McKinley
tsaghał	darkness
yeega'	spirits
nak'aghon	wolves
Miyeets	breath of life
Dołtoł	Moon

The Women in Old Parkas

snapping gunshot cold
blue stubborn lips clapped shut
the women in old parkas
loosen snares   intent & slow

they handle muskrat   Yukon way
appease his spirit *yeega'*
bare purple hands
stiffen   must set lines again

* * *

night drops quick black
in winterhouse   round shadows
cook fresh meat soup steam floats
thin bellies grumble

they pick up skinwork   squint
turn lamp-wick down   kerosene
almost gone   sew anyway

oh! this winter is the worst
everything running out not much furs
they make soft woman hum . . .

but hey! how about those new parkas
we hung up for Stick Dance!
how the people sing!
how crazy shadows dip and stamp
on dancehouse walls!   their
remembering arms rise like birdwings

* * *

at morning they look into sky
laugh at little lines of rain
finger their old parkas
think: spring is coming soon

Luci Tapahonso

I was born in Shiprock, New Mexico and am Navajo as can be—currently a graduate student at UNM and am pursuing a doctorate in Modern Literature this fall. Teaching a Native American Literature and Expository Writing also this fall. Most important of all, I am a mother of two daughters, Lori and Misty Dawn and married to "one of those Acomas"—Earl Ortiz.

the belly of the land

this road winds smooth
into the belly of the earth,
the rocks tinged blood-red,
cliffs bare and hard like ribs,
surround this place
dry and strong, sure as
children return.

this car wakes dust
swirling around, never ending
i can hardly see the
damp ditch weeds hovering over
the water there, clear
and cold in this hot dry land.

i still taste rain-fresh dirt
and good firm songs this land had given,
and returning prayers circle slow
and even into the belly of the land.

It was a Special Treat

Trips to Farmington were a special treat
when we were children.
Sometimes when we didn't get to go along,
we cried so hard that we finally had to draw straws
to decide fairly who got to go.
Always my oldest brother went because he drove,
my other brother went because he helped carry laundry,
my father went because he was the father,
and my mother went because she had the money and
knew where to go and what to buy.
And only one or two kids could go because we got in the way
and asked for stuff all the time.

We got up early on the Saturdays that we were going to town,
getting ready, sorting laundry
and gathering pop bottles that we turned in.
My father always checked the oil and tires on the pickup
and then he and my brothers would load up the big laundry tubs,
securing the canvas covers with heavy wooden blocks.
We would leave and the unfortunate ones who had to stay
home waved good-bye sullenly and the dogs chased the
truck down the road a ways before going home.

In Farmington, we would go to the laundry first.
It was always dark and clammy inside.
We liked pulling the clothes out of the wringer
even though my mother was nervous about letting us help.
After that, we went downtown and parked
in the free lot on the north side of Main Street.

Sometimes my father got off at the library and
we picked him up after we finished shopping.
Someone always had to "watch" the truck and
usually the one who made a nuisance of himself
at the laundry had to sit in the truck for two or
three hours while everyone else got to "see things"
around town.
If my father didn't go to the library—he stayed
in the truck and read the "Readers Digest" and
the kids were off the hook, naughty or not.

When we stopped at Safeway, which was our last stop,
it was early evening.
My mother would buy some bologna or cooked chicken
in plastic wrapped trays and a loaf of bread
to eat on the way home.
After the groceries were packed in securely,
under the canvas and blocks,
we loaded up again and started west to Shiprock.
We would eat and talk about who we saw,
what we should have bought instead of
what we did buy (maybe we can exchange it next time)
then the talking would slow down and by the time
we stopped at the Blue Window gas station,
everyone but my father was sleepy and tired.

He would start singing in Navajo in a clear, strong
voice and once in a while, my mother would ask him
about a certain song she heard once
"Do you know it, it was something like this..."
and she would sing a little, he would catch it
and finish the song while we listened half-asleep.

I whispered to my sister,
"He sings like those men on Navajo Hour,"
"It's so good." she said and
we went back to sleep until we reached home.

sheepherder blues

for Betty Holyan

"went to NCC for a year,"
she said,
"was alright.
there was some drinking, fights
i just kept low.
it was alright."

this friend
haven't see for a year or two.
it was a good surprise.
took her downtown
to catch the next bus
to Gallup.

"i went to Oklahoma City,"
she said,
"to vacation, visit friends,
have a good time.
but i got the sheepherder blues
in Oklahoma City."

"i kept worrying about my sheep
if they were okay
really missed them,
the long days in the sun.
so after 4 days
I had to leave Oklahoma City."

so she went back,
first bus to Gallup,
then a 2-hour drive
to her sheep.

Hills Brothers Coffee

my uncle is a small man
in navajo, we call him little uncle
        my mother's brother

he doesn't know english but
        his name in the white way is Tom Jim
        he lives about a mile or so
        down the road from our house.

one morning he sat in the kitchen
drinking coffee
        i just came over, he said
        the store is where i'm going to.
he tells me about how my mother seems to be gone
everytime he comes over.
        maybe she sees me coming
        then runs and jumps in her car
        and speeds away.
        he says smiling.
we both laugh just thinking of my mother
        jumping in her car and speeding.

i pour him more coffee and he spoons
        in sugar and creme until
        it looks almost like a chocolate shake
        then he sees the coffee can.
        oh, that's that coffee with
        the man in a dress, like a church man.
        ah-h-h, that's the one that does it for me.
        very good coffee.

i sit down and he tells me
        some coffee has no kick but
        this one is the one
        it does it good for me.

i pour us both a cup and while
        we wait for my mother
        his eyes crinkle with the smile
        and he says
        yes, oh yes, this is the very one.
        (putting in more sugar and creme.)
anyway,
i always buy hills brothers coffee
        once or sometimes twice a day
        i drink a hot coffee and

        it sure does it for me.

The Dust Will Settle

I

my grandmother
I cried to see you sitting
leaning against the hard strength
of the rocks when your strength
has failed you.

how is it that
we have come to this?
we are dirt-poor in a world
where land, sheep and songs
haunt us still.

the dusty smell of
gallup parking lots will be
the memories of the children—
their dreamless mights
long days waiting.

II

my uncle
you laugh too quick
and talk too loud yet
the children wait quietly watching
huddled in the pickup with
the 5-pound bag of oranges
you bought this morning.

they remember your voice
strong, clear on quiet nights
as you sang them to sleep easily.

we will wait.

III

what have i for you?
i curse my helplessness,
this frustration of having
nothing more than they.

i can cry and feel this hard anger
and know

grandmother
uncle

this will change
this will change

this winds will shift.
the dust will settle.

this will change.

Earle Thompson

I was born 13 March 1983 in Nespelem, Washington. I am a Native American of the Yakima Indian Nation. My father, Wilson was a Yakima and my mother, Isabelle, Yakima and Umatilla.

I attended schools on the Yakima Reservation and in Seattle, Washington, as well as others in the Northwest. However I did not graduate from high school, instead I received a G. E. D. I attended various colleges in the Northwest, this atmosphere and education provided me with the necessary tools to write and develop. Impractical as it may seem I began writing full time. I worked as a laborer, a clerk at United Airlines, mailhandler and clerk at U.S. Post Office.

I have been published in Blue Cloud Quarterly, Portland Review, Contact II, Seattle Times and the Northwest Indian News. On being Native American and writing, I feel: "My writing is like magic and I truly do not understand its nature. I use my heritage and non-native culture. Many individuals do not realize in our mythology Coyote, the trickster, created our tribe from stones on the shores of the Columbia tribe. As Coyote used stones to create, I use words to survive in harmony with my inner and outer nature.

Song****

Woman sits on her porch
knitting and begin singing
a Shakerhouse song:

> Hoy-hoy-ee ...
> Hoy-ee-hoy ...

Young Pah-tee-mah-ss rests
on the steps watching
a bough drifting inland
while the current tries taking
it to sea.
Cedar bough resists,
and in the boy's eyes
it becomes a dugout canoe—long,
with dark-haired men
naked to the waist paddling,
singing an old Lummi song.

Pah-tee-mah-ss and grandmother
watch seahawk dive from fine mist,
swoop upon a glint transformed
into fish

> Sudden splashing breaks
stillness of morning.

Winter Count of Sean Spotted Wolf

Sean Spotted Wolf examined the yellow-tinted
photograph of his family:
They stood facing the September sun and
the white walls of the Catholic school,
which made it appear clinical;

His grandparents were in the background of the
picture and his father and aunt stood in the
foreground.

Sheila, his aunt, was dressed in a checkered
dress, her dark hair in braids
and in her hands—she held a rosary.

In the sunlight, grandmother's brooch gleamed
and her flowered dress was ruffled in the breeze.
Spotted Eagle, his grandfather, held the blanket
tightly in his weathered hand and wore a necklace
made of grizzly bear claws.
Spotted Eagle's fur wraps made him
solemn and distant.

Sean Spotted Wolf imagined the scent of pines,
grass and the campfire—ancestral flames
curling into mythology.

As he lay back on the hospital bed, he could
feel and hear the crispness of the sheets;
in his brain, he recalled in spring the snow
melting around the fence posts and he had to
regain his breath. He coughed.

Sean Spotted Wolf remembered the elders had
taught him, if a person envisioned blue and
red horses galloping on the plains, before
their death;
Even then, yes—they will behold another sunrise.

Mythology

My grandfather placed wood
in the pot-bellied stove
and sat; he spoke:

"One time your uncle and me
seen some *stick-indians*
driving in the mountins
they moved along side
the car and watched us
look at them
they had long black hair
down their backs and were
naked
they ran past us."

Grandfather shifted
his weight in the chair.
He explained,
"*Stick-indians*
are powerful people
they come out during the fall.
They will trick little children
who don't listen
into the woods
and can imitate anything
so you should learn
about them."

Grandfather poured himself
a cup of coffee and continued;
"At night you should put tobacco
out for them
and whatever food you got
just give them some
cause *stick-indians*
can be vengeful
for people making fun of them.
They can walk through walls
and will stick a salmon up your ass for
laughing at them
this will not happen if you understand
and respect them."

My cousin giggled. I listened and remembered
Grandfather slowly sipped his coffee
and smiled at us.
The fire smouldered like
a volcano and crackled.
We finally went to bed.
I dreamt of the mountains;
and now
I understand my childhood.

Woman Made of Stars

For Susanne

Evening colours her amber breasts
drumming and singing could be heard
as the July moon tints
the tipis blue.

A Forty-Nine carries
on a summer breeze
and we listen to a pheasant
squawking in the distance.

My lover's skin forms
stars in the morning.

The Corral

The roan galloped
and steam rose slowly
from dilated nostrils,
mane shivering and rippling
with blood of the January sun.

Maples stood motionless
resembling skeletons
layered with icing

Speckled hoof pawing snow
for patches of snow.
Head arched, eyes glancing
toward the passing school bus.

Laura Tohe

I am Navajo, born and raised on the Navajo reservation in Arizona and New Mexico. When I was 15 I went to Albuquerque, NM to attend public school and to live at the BIA boarding school. The reason for leaving the reservation was that the closest school was 40 miles away from my home. Later I attended the University of New Mexico in Albuquerque where I received my bachelors degree.

Although I've lived in Albuquerque for many years and now Omaha, I consider them only as places where I've lived and not my home. It is the way I feel about the reservation—the land, the people and the culture—that makes it my home. I am from the reservation.

I am now attending graduate school at the University of Nebraska in Lincoln where I hope to get my Masters degree in Creative Writing in December 1983.

List of Publications: "Willow Man's Children," published in The Ceremony of Brotherhood Anthology, *Albuquerque, NM 1980. "A Gallup Cermonial Poem," published in* Ishmael Reed and Al Young's Quilt 1, *Oakland, CA 1981. "To Shimá sani," and "The Shooting," published in* Reciembra, *Espanola, NM 1982. "A Day at the Ceremonial," published in* Revista Rio Bravo, *Laredo, Texas, 1982.*

I have read my poetry and prose at UNM, The University of Albuquerque, the Indiana Pueblo Cultural Center, Barrio Vivo Series, Stables Gallery in Taos, NM, the Albuquerque Downtown Center for the Arts, Full Circle Bookstore and on KUNM FM Radio, Albuquerque, NM. I have also read for Native American Studies Spring Series at UNM and for the Arts in the Parks Program, Albuquerque, NM.

To Shimá sání

We called you Grandma Lupton
living among cedar and sagebrush

Ceremonial hogan facing east
Your house made of road signs
one side said "Steer"

Once, we took you to Gallup
to a pawn shop on Highway Sixty Six
Richardson's, I think

You'd never been to school
couldn't write your name
used your thumbprint as your signature

We went to Eagle cafe
you ate all the lettuce
took all the crackers
put them in your purse
said it was paid for
that was just your way

Mother of generations
you lived your life to the end of the season
returned to earth three winters ago
no one knows how old you were
you were born when the snow was this high

Stronger than many
even the Mexicans couldn't track you
as you hid under a sandstone ledge
heart thumping

You hitchhiked to Gallup
till your sight was nearly gone

Once I fell asleep in the cool dark hogan
earthy smell all around
feel of soft sheepskin
I was back in the womb

You came in and sat down
took off your moccasins

I wanted to ask you about your childhood
before the highway
before the railroad
before the Traders came

but the words stuck in my throat
only shameful silence followed

Now there is a memory on paper

The Shooting

Sarah T's husband shot her at the Tohatchi laundromat
while she unloaded the quilts from the pickup truck

he waited for her in an arroyo across the highway
under the russian olives
then took careful aim

she fell back
the laundry scattered at her feet

and the blood steamed red
all over the rocks

Sarah T's husband waited until the ambulance had gone
then pulled the last bullet on himself in a half-moon light

He said he didn't want to go alone

Cat or Stomp

to all the former cats and stomps
of the Navajo Nation

The first few days back at the Indian School
  after summer vacation
you wore your new clothes wrangler tight jeans stitched on the side
and boots (if you were lucky enough to have a pair)
Tony Lama
Nacona
or Acme
a true stomp listened to country western music   Waylon and George Jon
dying cowboy music and all that stuff

you wore
go go boots and bell bottoms if you were a cat and danced to the
Rolling Stones
even if you wore tennis shoes it was clear which side you were on

Every year the smoking greyhound buses pulled up in front of the old
gymnasium bringing loads of students
fresh off the reservation dragging metal trunks, train cases and
cardboard boxes precariously tied with string
the word spread quickly
of some new kid from Chinle or Many Farms
"is he a cat or stomp?" someone would ask
"Stomp"
and those with appropriate clothing would get their chance to
dance with him that night

Female Rain

Female Rain
        Dancing from the south
            cloudy cool and gray
                    pregnant with rain child

At dawn she gives birth to a gentle mist
flowers bow with wet sustenance
                    luminescence all around

Male Rain

Male Rain
        He comes riding a dark horse
                angry malevolent cold
            bringing floods and heavy winds
Warrior rain   having a 49 night
            then rides away leaving
                his enemy behind

At Mexican Springs

Up here I can see the
    glimmering lights of Gallup calling the reservation
    like a whore standing under a light post
    the way they do in Juarez
    in Gallup when our sons are born they say,
        "she gave birth to a wino."
    Gallup steals our children
    returns them empty and crumbled

But here the hills are quietly breathing
    the earth is a warm glowing blanket
    holding me in her arms
        It is here among the sunset in
                every plant
                every rock
                every shadow
                every movement
                every thing
      I relive visions of ancient stories
        First Woman and First Man
        their children stretched across these eternal sandstones

    a deep breath
    she brings me sustenance
    life
and I will live to tell my children these things.

mah-do-ge tohee

mah-do-ge tohee is a member of the Oto-Ioway tribe of Oklahoma. Formerly an associate editor of A Magazine, *he currently edits* Coyote On the Turtle's Back, *a publication of the Institute of American Indian Arts. His writings have appeared in* A Magazine, Spawning the Medicine River, *and* Plenty Onions. *He currently resides in Santa Fe, New Mexico.*

indian america

they're selling tickets to the sundance
they're selling beaded knives & forks
beneath the sacred peaks
an indian band was playing a marching tune,
it looked funny to see
an old navajo man in traditional dress
wearing thick, dark-rimmed glasses
playing the trombone

2

down the avenue,
an old, beat-up one-eyed ford
comes rattling around the corner
as snow falls nonchalant
in front of a local hock shop
christmas lights are blinking off & on
in the background
spelling out,
"nixon had it coming"
as the driver turns off the ignition,
the engine coughs & kicks,
sputters for a few moments
then backfires & slowly dies
two twentieth-century blurry-eyed winter babes
lug out an old black & white t.v.
moments later,
they emerge from the hock shop all smiles
before they get in, one says,
"hey! this back tire is real low,
we better get some air into it quick!"
"ok." the driver says, "hop in."
half a block down,
they pull into the drive-up window
of a local liquor store,
stock up, & drive away

3

in jicarilla, the apaches run their own bar.

258

agnes

coyote kicks back,
bringing us here. . .to this moment
& his hair is just as long as hers,
they even speak the same language,
only their clan is different

today, coyote's a bourbon indian
living in some ghetto
outside of pearl's harbor
beachfront

yesterday, leonard crow dog & fritz scholder
were cussing each other out
when coyote appeared with his woman
crow dog & scholder fell silent
when coyote farted in their direction
winked, smiled & strolled astray

in her anxiety,
she was last seen driving
a two-tone fifty-four rambler
heading towards red rock,
she had a price to pay
& she was late

in some obscure beachfront bar,
sitting with his reflector shades,
coyote sips a tequila sunset,
yawns & passes out
muttering. . .agnes. . .agnes

untitled

we sat in an old, crumbling house
a group of vagabonds—wanderers
we talked politics & rolled numbers
we talked religion & dropped acid
at the same time,
a friend of mine was dancing
to the beat of the drum
with bearclaws hooked to his bleeding chest,
sage tied to his wrists
an eagle feather's braided into his hair
he could smell the river that flowed
over a mile & a half away
before he fell
into his visions
perched on the top of the center pole,
an eagle peered into his suffering eyes & screamed

an eagle carries his heart across the sky. . .

legends
starving on the rez
colors clash in the night
where
will we ride?

Gerald Vizenor

Gerald Vizenor is an enrolled member of the Minnesota Chippewa Tribe, White Earth Reservation, of Anishinabe (Chippewa) and French descent. His poems have been published in numerous anthologies and journals, including Voices of the Rainbow *(Viking), edited by Kenneth Rosen.*

Vizenor has also published several books about tribal cultures: The Everlasting Sky: New Voices from the People Named the Chippewa *(Macmillan),* Wordarrows: Indians and Whites in the New Fur Trade *(University of Minnesota Press),* Summer in the Spring *(Nodin Press), a collection of traditional Anishinabeg songs and stories,* Tribal Scenes and Ceremonies *(Nodin Press), a collection of articles and essays, and* Earthdivers: Tribal Narratives of Mixed Descent *(University of Minnesota Press), his most recent book.*

Vizenor has worked as an organizer in urban tribal communities, as a journalist for the Minneapolis Tribune, and as a teacher. He has taught at Bemidji State University, University of California at Berkeley, and at the University of Minnesota where he currently teaches American Indian Studies.

Vizenor has published one novel, Darkness in Saint Louis Bearheart *(Truck Press); he is currently working on a new novel.*

White Earth Reservation 1980

Intersections

1
the late october sun
slides through the cottonwood trees

2
tribal tricksters
roam on the rearview mirror
dreamleaps
mixedbloodtwists
backwards on the old government roads

colonial remembrance cards
captured trees
cultures closed for the season

federal agents
hunker low on carrion crow

beaded crucifixion
healers doubled over in the reeds
secrets poisoned
scouts bare the sacred on a sash

3
culture cultists
sound the color lines at pine point
count canoes
wrecked in the wild rice wars

soldiers in unmarked graves
spirit scorched
general allotment stumps
tinted plastics
crack on a cold clear night

4
high on the trail of words
new shamans collared at the centerfolds
medicine bundles
stashed in circular files

5
the river moons
bound over the bridge
stone faces gather the light
witnesses at last
the roads to white earth are paved

6
fiscal storms
close the tribal survival schools

reporters chart the cuts
civil scores
whitemen save the late movies

reservation children
cast their bodies to the cold buses
corporate sports
john locke
invented histories
shadows seep from the concrete

7
lake itasca dancers
ten thousand winters at the woodland rim
tribal families
bearwalks at the source
northern lights
where schoolcraft soaked his feet

8
animals at the treelines
dubious totems
cheated outback in colonial furs
blessed by the jesuits
one word removed from snowmobiles
send back the traps and hats

9
the biomedical man
impeached the faces on a medicine drum
runs a white thunderbird
winded over the reservation

returning from a moose hunt
he buried his name at a public health curve

10
mission ruins
cower on a meadow near bad medicine lake
toilet doors
stations of the cross
pale litanies
down in the bright weeds
tribal touchwood at the seams

Indians at the Guthrie

wounded american indian
decorated with invented names
trade beads
federal contract numbers
pinups from national geographic
limps past the guthrie theater

wounded american indian
stops at attention on a plastic leg
salutes with the wrong hand
blonde children
crossing in purple tapestries
review their castles
barricades on stage with reservation plans

rehearsing overscreams from sand creek
flesh burned at mystic river
frozen ghost dancers
wounded tribes at wounded knee

hearts down in spiritual wars
summers overnight
sterno at dawn in bemidji
poison wine in gallop
cultural suicides downtown on the reservations

wounded american indian
decorated with invented names
salutes with the wrong hand

theater treaties end in the dark
actors mountup
ride beside the buffalo bills of kenwood
cultural westerns
new parties in the corporate hills

Minnesota Camp Grounds

white armies
claim the woodland lakes

summer sorties
near the precious triangle
walker
park rapids
bemidji
praise aluminum and ice
plastic flowers

butterflies
dead on the grill of a brown camero

earthfascists
chop dope
deep down in tribal graves

imprisoned deer
cut low whistle grass overnight

rivers descend
postcards close at dark centerfolds

culture warders
blink their power lights
cite nude swimmers
move the outside toilets
back from the dead lake water
one at a time

Auras on the Interstates

follow the trickroutes
homewardbound in darkness

noise tired
from the interstates

trucks whine through our families
places of conception

governments raze
half the corners we have known

houses uprooted
sacred trees deposed
municipal machines
plow down our generation vines
tribal doorshapes

condominium cultures
foam low
stain the rivers overnight

thin auras
hold our space in dreams
cut the interstates
from the stoop
bedroom window ruins

noise tired
we are laced in dark arms
until morning

Holiday Inn at Bemidji

famous animals
spoke here
birds once celebrated this tribal place
centuries before the carpets
sculptured industrial pile
polymer furniture
flocked walls
motel red
dead on the inside

windigos curse here now
perched in plastic birch trees

new world colonies
dress for lunch in resin shirts
fluorescent burned
shamanless
weak earthbeat
pinched in rows around the indoor pool
chicken feeders
seasoned with chlorine

new world colonists
voted this morning to block the sun
save the carpet color
molded orchards in the concrete

Photo by Lois Welch

James Welch

Blackfeet on his father's side and Gros Ventre on his mother's, James Welch was born in 1940 in Browning, Montana. He attended schools on the Blackfeet and Fort Belknap reservations in Montana and received his B.A. from the University of Montana.

His books include two highly praised novels from Harper and Row: WINTER IN THE BLOOD and THE DEATH OF JIM LONEY and a collection of poems, RIDING THE EARTHBOY 40, reissued by Harper and Row in 1976. James Welch has served on the Literature Panel of the National Endowment for the Arts and on the Montana State Board of Pardons.

"I have seen works written about Indians by whites ... but only an Indian knows who he is. If he has grown up on a reservation he will naturally write about what he knows. And hopefully he will have the toughness and fairness to present his material in a way that is not manufactured by conventional stance. Whites have to adopt a stance; Indians already have one."

Harlem, Montana:
Just Off the Reservation

We need no runners here. Booze is law
and all the Indians drink in the best tavern.
Money is free if you're poor enough.
Disgusted, busted whites are running
for office in this town. The constable,
a local farmer, plants the jail with wild
raven-haired stiffs who beg just one more drink.
One drunk, a former Methodist, becomes a saint
in the Indian church, bugs the plaster man
on the cross with snakes. If his knuckles broke,
he'd see those women wail the graves goodbye.

Goodbye, goodbye, Harlem on the rocks,
so bigoted, you forget the latest joke,
so lonely, you'd welcome a battalion of Turks
to rule your women. What you don't know,
what you will never know or want to learn—
Turks aren't white. Turks are olive, unwelcome
alive in any town. Turks would use
your one dingy park to declare a need for loot.
Turks say bring it, step quickly, lay down and
    dead.

Here we are when men were nice. This photo,
    hung
in the New England Hotel lobby, shows them
    nicer
than pie, agreeable to the warring bands of red-
    skins
who demanded protection money for the price of
    food.
Now, only Hutterites out north are nice. We hate
them. They are tough and their crops are always
    good.
We accuse them of idiocy and believe their belief
    all wrong.

Harlem, your hotel is overnamed, your children
are raggedy-assed but you go on, survive
the bad food from the two cafes and peddle
your hate for the wild who bring you money.
When you die, if you die, will you remember
the three young bucks who shot the grocery up,
locked themselves in and cried for days, we're
    rich,
help us, oh God, we're rich.

Thanksgiving at Snake Butte

In time we rode that trail
up the butte as far as time
would let us. The answer to our time
lay hidden in the long grasses
on the top. Antelope scattered

through the rocks before us, clattered
unseen down the easy slope to the west.
Our horses balked, stiff-legged,
their nostrils flared at something unseen
gliding smoothly through brush away.

On top, our horses broke, loped through
a small stand of stunted pine, then jolted
to a nervous walk. Before us lay
the smooth stones of our ancestors, the fish,
the lizard, snake and bent-kneed

bowman—etched by something crude,
by a wandering race, driven by their names
for time: its winds, its rain, its snow
and the cold moon tugging at the crude figures
in this, season of their loss.

D-Y Bar

The tune is cowboy; the words, sentimental crap.
Farther out, wind is mending sagebrush,
stapling it to earth in rows only a badger
would recommend. Reservoirs are dry,
the sky commands a cloud high
to skip the Breaks bristling with heat
and stunted pine.

In stunted light, Bear Child tells a story
to the mirror. He acts his name out,
creeks muscling gorges fill his glass
with gumbo. The bear crawls on all fours
and barks like a dog. Slithering snake-wise
he balances a nickel on his nose. The effect,
a snake in heat.

We all know our names here. Summer is a poor
season to skip this place or complain
about marauding snakes. Often when wind
is cool off mountains and the flats
are green, cars stop for gas, motors clicking
warm to songs of a junction bar, head down,
the dormant bear.

Surviving

The day-long cold hard rain drove
like sun through all the cedar sky
we had that late fall. We huddled
close as cows before the bellied stove.
Told stories. Blackbird cleared his mind,
thought of things he'd left behind, spoke:

"Oftentimes, when sun was easy in my bones,
I dreamed of ways to make this land."
We envied eagles easy in their range.
"That thin girl, old cook's kid, stripped naked
for a coke or two and cooked her special stew
round back of the mess tent Sundays."
sparrows skittered through the black brush.

That night the moon slipped a notch, hung
black for just a second, just long enough
for wet black things to sneak away our cache
of meat. To stay alive this way, it's hard. . . .

In My Lifetime

This day the children of Speakthunder
run the wrong man, a saint unable
to love a weasel way, able only to smile
and drink the wind that makes the others go.
Trees are ancient in his breath.
His bleeding feet tell a story of run
the sacred way, chase the antelope naked
till it drops, the odor of run
quiet in his blood. He watches cactus
jump against the moon. Moon is speaking
woman to the ancient fire. Always woman.

His sins were numerous, this wrong man.
Buttes were good to listen from. With thunder-
hands his father shaped the dust, circled
fire, tumbled up the wind to make a fool.
Now the fool is dead. His bones go back
so scarred in time, the buttes are young to look
for signs that say a man could love his fate,
that winter in the blood is one sad thing.

His sins—I don't explain. Desperate in my song,
I run these woman hills, translate wind
to mean a kind of life, the children of
   Speakthunder
are never wrong and I am rhythm to strong
   medicine.

Roberta Hill Whiteman

What have I done for the last five years? I wrote some of the poems in my first collection with the help of a NEA fellowship, taught at the Oneida Tribal School for a while, more recently, presented a paper at MLA this past December on Contemporary American Indian Poetry, and gave readings at Cooper Union in New York; Bemidgi State University in Minnesota; the University of South Dakota; Oklahoma Arts Council; Eugene, Oregon; and the University of Wisconsin—Stout and LaCrosse. This month I will be reading here at the University of Wisconsin— Eau Claire and at Waukesha.

I have a difficult time gathering the events in my life together. For a long time, I lived in a hall of mirrors. Each mirror reflected shadow and wind, trees and creeks, rooms and scents, those I have loved who are dead or lost and those I have loved who have disappeared or have gone insane. As I look in each mirror, I know consciously I was there, but over time, those reflections take on more beauty, distance and pain and I cannot always recognize the self who was there. It is like a crow flying in sunlight. When I see the crow in the tree, I know it is black. The crow with sunlight reflecting a sheen in its feathers shines white.

Three years ago I married Ernest Whiteman and with our three children, Jacob, 8; Heather, 7; and Melissa, 6, we moved to Eau Claire, where I was to teach at the University, and Ernie was to finish a Bachelor of Fine Arts Degree. The years in this mirror have broken into the space of the hall itself and have given me a sense of wholeness and balance unknown before. Teaching English Composition, American Indian Literature, and Creative Writing, I've become more aware of the dimensions and power of language and the visual arts. Ernie and I share our enthusiasm for the Arts and talk about how the world has tilted toward the desire to force growth, gain power and control and lose the connections to the earth and sky which sustain us. We remind each other how important a sense of connection to the earth and sky is, how necessary our humility before their power, and how we must see with the eye of the heart to be happy. Such themes are part of my first collection, Star Quilt, to be published this year by Holy Cow! Press of Minneapolis. Ernie offered to do the cover design and sketches; Jim Perlman has been a wonderful editor.

I have a number of other projects going—more poems, a few short stories and a novel I keep plugging away at. So much tyranny stalks through the world today— tyranny of the marketplace and of the heart. Mayans are being massacred in Guatemala, unemployment and alcoholism continue to kill us on our reservations, radiation poisoning and acid rain kill our means of life, sky and earth wounded again and again. The only strength I find comes from the myths of our people. As in the Popul Vuh, I believe it is the artisan's responsibility to help the earth overcome such dreadful tyranny. It is the artisan's responsibility to sing the sky clear so that we can walk across the earth, in a place fit for flowers.

In the Longhouse, Oneida Museum

House of five fires, you never raised me.
Those nights when the throat of the furnace
wheezed and rattled its regular death,
I wanted your wide door,

your mottled air of bark and working sunlight,
wanted your smokehole with its stars,
and your roof curving its singing mouth above me.
Here are the tiers once filled with sleepers,

and their low laughter measured harmony or strife.
Here I could wake amazed at winter,
my breath in the draft a chain of violets.
The house I left as a child now seems

a shell of sobs. Each year I dream it sinister
and dig in my heels to keep out the intruder
banging at the back door. My eyes burn
from cat urine under the basement stairs

and the hall reveals a nameless hunger,
as if without a history, I should always walk
the cluttered streets of this hapless continent.
Thinking it best I be wanderer,

I rode whatever river, ignoring every zigzag,
every spin. I've been a fragment, less than my name,
shaking in a solitary landscape,
like the last burnt leaf on an oak.

What autumn wind told me you'd be waiting?
House of five fires, they take you for a tomb,
but I know better. When desolation comes,
I'll hide your ridgepole in my spine

and melt into crow call, reminding my children
that spiders near your door
joined all the reddening blades of grass
without oil, hasp or uranium.

Midwinter Stars

The trees across the street have loved me
in your absence. The Pole star, caught by branches
of the front yard elm, blurs
when I look at it directly and passes
through midwinter slower than other stars.
Whenever you came by, the forest

filled with signs. A pocket in soft grass
meant resting deer. Hoofprints in the sand
lead through brush and fallen leaves
to even dimmer trails. I hated all my rooms.
The lonely light, absurd.
I warmed your shoulders one late November storm

and trees sang in minor chords.
Aware of dawn before it came, you woke,
smiled into clothes, juggled with coffee,
then drove away. I watched shadows turn
from indigo to grey.
Like other obsessions, this will change,

yet my arm was happy, numb
with all your weight. I learned the easy signs:
cloud cover, tracking snow.
I fell with every flake and wanted to drape
over trees, into city blocks, on those corners
where you bought beer, over cars and bridges

in that namesake of despair.
There are places I have never felt at ease,
where something taps against the glass,
the blackjack of a cop and bitter lives.
Who the hunter? Who the hunted? Who survives?
This cold circuit wobbles without rest.

I never could accept beginning or end.
You'll find on the other side of winter
crocus trembling in a bountiful dawn.
I plan to join the deer,
for in this dark, the trees bar my window
and not one shadow moves.

Notes for Albuquerque

"There is a screw loose
in the public machinery somewhere."
Schoolcraft on the BIA, 1828

I

Threads spiral toward a center,
turn on fingers of freezing children.
One boy ran, scared by routine, a glaring sun.
Hiding three days,
they found him blistered.
He fell asleep in Math, stupid.
Call him a fire-eyed coyote,
a berry in the paw of a bear.
"Cut the heat
in Arizona. It's warm there."

II

Beware of wind.
Apache nights dry the morning. Why hatred
in Ronan? They watch Red Sky Sun Down
make an x. Her knowledge could protect
the bees. "We must help the boarding schools,
get water from Gila Community,
dam it in the mountains."
No rain in three years. Phoenix thrives.

III

A man was promoted today. Now an assistant commissioner
dreams of junior high and Shakespeare.
"Dark skinned savages with wailing songs."
Dimpled girls once teased his stutter.
He no longer listens. Children are sick
in Santa Rosa; at Salt River,
work Math on toilet paper.

IV

Lose this hurt,
a trestle lost to canyons. Our ground
is now legend. Dew smokes along
Ska na wis. The circle of meeting trees
north of the Lawrence gives way to moss.
Children are sick in Santa Rosa.
We give away to this deepening thunder.
The sand knows lizards and coyotes.
Only owls have homes.

Woman Seed Player

for Oscar Howe

You balanced her within a cyclone
and I believe the young wind
that frequents the graveyard
tugs her sleeve. Her hand never wavers,
though the stakes are always high.

When running shadow turns rattler,
her concern is how the mountain rises
beyond its line of sorrow. Then,
shooting her seeds, she bids
the swallow fly over rolling hills.

I have been obsessed with permanence.
Struggling in that open space under every word,
I've heard exuberant waves drift
denying limitations. Last April
when we trudged upstairs

to where we found you sketching,
you said no one had ever gone full circle,
from passion through pattern and back again
toward pebbles moist with moonlight.
How easily the rain cross-stitches

a flower on the screen, quickly
pulls the threads, varying the line.
Many times this year, I've watched that player
play. She doesn't force the day
to fit her expectations.

Now she pulls me through.
The leaf light dust and her stable hand
allow my will its corner of quiet.
Watch dust embracing the nervous wheat;
every throw's a different combination.

Dust whirs brighter in the door jam,
one last uproar before the rain.
Her bundle contains and yet foregoes
the dark dust already fallen for tomorrow
from long since gentle stars.

The title and subject come from a picture by Oscar Howe.

Night along the Mackinac Bridge

I wait to tangle fear around my hand
like fire, to hold your owl's eyes with mine.
Lake Michigan dries sweat from magic,
squeezes belief into the world. Jacob runs
away the night as beer crackles down his jeans.
My past rustles offshore, a sail only rowboats watch.

I return to kin I've avoided fifteen years,
and find my skin's never felt so much at home.
That cinnamon wrapping would tear
from schools where Jesuits waged revenge.
Near Oneida, geese gather over fields, fewer now
bound for Labrador. Last year, you left with them.

I'll unravel black hair, shape mongoloid folds,
always be stupid about the songs. Like a miller
burned by bulbs, I remember stillness
behind the faded blind, a light that hummed
my shoulders into fire. What was once so distant
breaks upon me now, while dark water crumbles the moon.

Photo by Elizabeth Woody

Phyllis Wolf

Phyllis Wolf, Assiniboine-Ojibwa, was born on the Fort Peck Reservation in Montana. Her first poems were published in the American Poetry Review and she has since published in numerous literary journals, including the Greenfield Review's Native American Writings Issue.

Akawense

Grandfather has three sparks
he calls to through a tunnel
of sand. As day darkens they come
out singing, shooting one after
one from sand, giving Grandfather fresh
medicine.

Louie's leg stretches each day
until skin is so tight
he screams when touched.

Sparks come to him saying that they
will not give life to one who worships
cloth. "But Louie is Shinabbee," Grand
father says. They tell him *No. Sick
blood will reach the heart that
sings for cloth. Leave the man who is*

neither. They dart back into the tunnel.
Grandfather smooths
sand and walks home.

Across the lake two sisters toll
a death. Grandfather looks to
the church nearly choked by birch.
                                    Tying
his canoe to the landing, he follows
those that carry Louie. . .

Grandfather has been away many
nights. His eyes are rimmed in red.
He calls to his three, but they won't
sing from sand.
                        His lips are cracked
as he slumps over his chest. Then
he hears them come, shooting one
after one into dark. *We said to leave
that man, Akawense. . . You didn't
listen. We'll sing no more. We each
give you a moon.*

Grandfather smooths out
footprints.

Manomin*

Gathered under leaded
skies and packed sometimes
in webbed feet of duck or skin
of fawn we waited for you
to be steamed. And ate
you slowly, remembering
dog-eaters who died
with Ojibwas tasting
manomin on blackened tongue.

*Ojibwa for rice that grows wild.

Lac Courte Orielles: 1936

It follows me
fifteen miles—eyes catching mine.
Traces my steps, hovering elm to elm.
Spiny tail, feathers quiver
he is laughing...
Black eyes seek my red
heart, he does not see my gun readied.
I pivot, the gun rings out, laughter
deep in his throat never comes nearer.
I do, to see its tongue
black as his eyes
drop from his beak
six inches...

I walk home

drums beat, women wail:
Charley is dead
with a tongue black as his eyes
laying on his hairless chest
inches of it.

Rolling Thunder

for Norman

Much tobacco is burnt.

Around his head dark bodies
cease to wail. His pain
becomes the ripples on the lake he
wakes to every morning. Sweet
tobacco fills his head.
                    Rolling
thunder covers with violet
brief spaces of sun left
on the desert. Warm whispers
touch my palm. Together we've
burnt much tobacco, Grand
father. See the clouds
become deeper as they pass the rise.

Midewiwan

Bad Luck After Conversion

Crumbling a dark leaf between darker fingers,
he throws the grain to earth and bends closer to see
a pattern.
        A cold wind combs his wings as he flies over
stone-cellared farmhouses. Below he eyes a purple
flower growing close to wild blueberries.
                          His throat
burns as he swallows purple dye, but when waking with
morning all pain has been purged.
                 *

He felt warm breath of the frock
near his ear, whispering
it was his magic that killed
her. Eyes fall to strong fingers that once
held a steaming cup to her lips.
Beside him stood the solemn frock. He held it
begging forgiveness.
              *

A beaver pouch clung
to the side of one man of the Lodge. At his
he found a silver cross.
              *

The stomach bites itself. He writhes from pain.
Reciting a prayer, he stops and looks to the window.
                    Flying
he finds an herb.
              Taking his pouch from a box
the leaves sour
at his nose as the drawstring is loosened. Voices
are long in coming. Although snow
makes rooms whiter, his is black.
Drinking the liquid, voices become stronger.
He sees them that sing one strain.
             *

Coming from the heated Lodge, a man who
sings from beaver cannot stop the sweat
that runs from his eyes and opened palms.

282

Elizabeth Woody

I am from a Sahaptin Woman and a Dine' Man. Born for the Todachinii. walked in the womb through Canyon De Chelly to my winter birth in '59. My mother claims to have heard the icicles sing while I was born.

For telling me this I am grateful. She taught me the simplest mechanics for singing internally. The fragmented intuitive thoughts that arise and resemble poetry and allude to the actuality. My poetry seems inadequate impostor from this first speech. She has told me how closely she resembles a poet.

As an artist I have studied with my Grandparents in Warm Springs, Oregon. We would spend hours driving someplace "Just to Look, cuz it's so beautiful." We walked in Lava Beds, visited mouths of rivers where fish would jump for you if you threw in bread. We would pick spots near mountains to listen to the wind and wait for deer. My Grandmother would feel the presence of deer and knew how to find them. My Grandfather could feel the start of a good joke in the air and knew where to find your laughter.

Points of reference are helpful:

I have studied in Japan. Traveling the country I gathered up the roots of my many habits. Being in a different culture clarified my own. I found the immutable essences of their past tucked away in refined boundaries. These essences exist as soft sensitivities and of a harshness in the people. They are on a bigger reservation than we are here in America. They have handled the fences around their tradition and art.

Other influences I have felt are from my past encounters with poets. I've listened to Sandra McPherson, James Welch and Primus St. John in Portland, Oregon. They gave me the taste for poetry. Needing more stimulation I moved from the Northwest to Santa Fe. I enrolled at the Institute of American Indian Arts in Creative Writing under Phil Foss. This seemed to be at the blossoming of the program with several young poets. At this time I learned from every one some detail and nature of the "Art of Writing" that doesn't exist in the class work. Living in brief asylum I have discovered how to add depth to my work.

I am graduating from I.A.I.A. in May, 1983. I feel that I have come to another type of graduation, one from my adolescent pretenses of what poetry and art should be. Poetry is my greater, creative intuition and saves delicate life every day.

Black Fear

Pointing, his face looked at the blackened windows.
The boat was stripped of shine,
old and blackened with paint.
Electrical tape on chrome.
"Renegades" echoing in his mind.

Explanation of renegades is hinted,
never known fully, until
you are blackened in the act, in night
as illegal fisherman.

Dark treads in water
On watch in pitch black.
Sleeping on fish scales.
Fish, eye to eye,
No engine, oars lapping the nets in.
Fear, in the darkness, the river's depths undone.

The river's depths undone into fishermen's nets,
moistly tickling their backs.
Unwound like an Indian woman's hair,
full and soft down her back,
touching the child in bed.

The fear is to find dark hair clinging to illegal
silver scaled on the sides of a fish.
The fear is to see the police trespass
on other people's land to break
the Indian renegade's fingers,
leaving darkly bruised, the man.

In Impressions of Hawk Feathers
Willow Leaves Shadow

Sun sets on a bright blameless wall a barrage of rays.
Rattles dance as gusted blows and reprieves.
My youthful face, the lean hint to my current mask,
lies on the floor. A painfully addressed note
of conscience from a lover I onced pursued.
A picture taken by him with my camera, a simple vow.

I had insisted the sacred in voice would prevail.
The moon glistens higher, nighted in cerulean blue.
Moon outside, receiving remembered songs,
Soliloquies dead.

The sunset voice calls again,
a moan, "Where are you child?"
A dead mother wails passionately
to my ears from my window.
the crystal tomb shields the transitions of my moods.
I seal my past with my deprivations.
The dead have yet to awaken within, giving new life
to the ravaged coil. The spiral of I'm...
the DNA structure of color, new child.
The deep clip of a door shuts somewhere.
Inside one keens and throes alone.
The cry is my own, the force of breath
the last blossoms to grow.

Custer Must Have Learned to Dance

I am caught in the new power
of his dedicated motion.
Rolling in the calvary money,
playing in the hands of Indian children,
I become an Origami object
of horses, teepees, and men.
They warp into vans, trendy clothes
and books on religious attitudes
to the dying planet.
I am taught within this nation
ideals of Greek platitudes;
an odyssey of epitomal frustrations.
Original sin, archetypes and eternity
become obsessions of dusty libidos.
Freud interlocks with the loss
of the national inclinations
birthing aboriginal psychosis.

Eagles

For the Taos Journey

Yellow paper planes fly
pirouetting in pinwheel circles
carrying ciphered spirituals.
Sighing in wind
they unfold and lie in bare patterns.
One message from each soul above
clutching the bridge and dangerous edge.
In the tongue tickings of words
the flight becomes inaudible
stalks of paper eagles.
It flies. It round dances.
Farewell and our hearts
lie out there
touched once
and flown.
The writings sleep in intimate
destinations,
reigned, yet wild, un-named.
Downstream we cover in Indian blankets
touched gray with smoke
trilling the mass poetic flight.
An eagle whistles upon us.
People birthed, flown and earth caught.
A mirage to the one above.
A protective shadow slides the canyon's coolness
in prisms of water.
We melt as lather and return
to our bodies with river
sighs and current.
We've flown and landed.
The eagle waves away
turning the earth
as an edge in the sky.

Night Crackles

Darkness refuses the amnesia
of rough pictographs.
A honeycomb buzzes incessantly.
My heartbeat grows
a count into millions.
The ritual night encounters
weave sleep.
The dog pants,
sensing the sun
flushing the eastern face,
smiling a thin wire of horizon.
Tall, brittle grasses
sing in a dance with wind.
It strikes my hair.
I sleep, yet hear.
I dream, but know this happens.
I feel, yet touch nothing.
I know the night
undaunted, relates location
to the sun.

Ray A. Young Bear

Ray Young Bear is a member of the Mesquakie tribe, formerly known as Sauk and Fox. Born November 12, 1950, he has been writing since 1966. Widely anthologized and published frequently in literary magazines, he is the author of a book of poetry, WINTER OF THE SALAMANDER (Harper and Row, 1980). To quote from the jacket notes: "Ray Young Bear began thinking his poems in his native tongue then translating them verbatim. Through ten years of writing he has refined his technique so that the poems while no longer word-for-word translations have become, in essence, an authentic Native American experience, finalized in English." He currently is living in the Mesquakie settlement in Tama, Iowa and putting together an anthology of traditional stories from the Midwest.

grandmother

if i were to see
her shape from a mile away
i'd know so quickly
that it would be her.
the purple scarf
and the plastic
shopping bag.
if i felt
hands on my head
i'd know that those
were her hands
warm and damp
with the smell
of roots.
if i heard
a voice
coming from
a rock
i'd know
and her words
would flow inside me
like the light
of someone
stirring ashes
from a sleeping fire
at night.

in the first place of my life

in the first place of my life
something which comes before all others
there is the sacred and holylike
recurring memory of an old teethless
bushy white-haired man
gesturing with his wrinkled hands
and squinty eyes for me to walk to him
sitting on the edge of his wooden
summer bed

being supported and guided along
like a newborn spotted fawn
who rises to the cool and minty wind
i kept looking at his yellow
and cracked fingernails
they moved back and forth against the stove
and they shined against the kerosene
                                    darkened
kitchen and bedroom walls

i floated over the floor towards him
and he smiled as he lifted me up to the
                                    cardboard
ceiling and on there were symbols i later read
as that of emily
her scratched-in name alongside the face
of a lonely softball player

remembrance two: it was shortly after he
                                    held me
or else it was a day
or a couple of months

or a couple of years later when i saw him next
the bodies of three young men leaned against him
as he staggered out towards the night

i never knew what closed him
why i never saw him again
he was on the floor with a blanket
over his still and quiet body
above me there was a mouth moving
it was the face of a woman who had opened
the door for the three young men
she pointed to his body
this is your grandfather

and then i remember the daylight
with the bald-headed man in overalls
he too mentioned the absence
of my grandfather
i understood them both

i picture the appletree and its shade
as he was talking to me i saw a group
of people on the green grass
on the ground were table and linen cloths
with bowls and dishes of fruits and meats

the bald-headed man in overalls stood
in the brilliance of the summer daylight
his eyebrows made his face look concerned
or worried

later he stood on the same grass
he had been chosen to fill my grandfather's
empty place

the new colored blankets around his waist
and chest glistened with the fresh
fibrous wool
the beads reflected the good weather
the earth and its people stood and danced
with the beautifully clothed man
who was my grandfather
standing in between time
watching the daylight pass through
his eyes

from then on i only saw him occasionally
he would stand on his tractor
waving to each passing car on the road
as he drove home from
the soybean fields
or else he would converse with my two uncles
that the blood which ran through their
father's veins
and theirs was unlike the rest of the tribe
in that it came from the beginnings
unlike ours

one chip of human bone

one chip of human bone

it is almost fitting
to die on the railroad tracks.

i can easily understand
how they felt on their long
staggered walks back

grinning to the stars.

there is something about
trains, drinking, and being
an indian with nothing to lose.

poem for viet nam

i will always miss the feeling
of friday on my mind.
the umbrella somewhere
in the dumps of south
viet nam. in exchange
for candy it will hide
the helicopter.
franco must be here
in a guy's heart. i've
heard so much about him.
the closest i got was when
i machine-gunned
the people waist deep
inside the brown speckled
swamp. the castle where we drank
the sweet wine from giant fish bowls
has come against us. we knew that
when we killed them they tasted
the blood of whoever stood
beside them. some of us
thought of our families.
the cactus warms in our
bodies. the old mansion
where his friend played
cards has murdered his
brother and we see the stabbing
right through the door. while
i ran i made a song from
my wind. i have not held
this god beside me. only
this rock that i've often
heard about stays and at times
feel it must be true. his words
are like my dreams. they are eating
balls of rice in front of us.
i heard them talking a couple
of yards ahead of us. the jets flew
in v formation and they reminded me
of the wild ducks back home. once,
when i looked down, my wrists opened
and i wiped the blood on a tree.
i can only sit there and imagine.
they were ear close. the next day
i wore their severed fingers
on my belt. my little brother
and i hunted while someone close
was being buried on the same hill
where we will end. we hardly knew him,
coming into his family twelve years
too late. it was a time when
strawberries came bearing
no actual meanings. the bright
color of our young clothes walks

292

out from the fog. a house speaks
through the mouth and mind
of the silversmith. we saw the red
sand on his boots. what do we
remember of him? i remember he
said good-bye that one fall.
it was on a sunday. he was slender.
the burns from a rifle barrel spotted
half his face. april black is somewhere.
i scratched his back knowing
of sacrifices. the children
growing up drunk.

the last dream

the old man was already well ahead
of the spring, singing the songs
of his clan as well as others,
trying to memorize each segment
and each ritual, the differences
of the first-born, who would drink
the water from the drum, why it
was hard teaching the two-legged
figurine to connect itself
to the daylight, wondering
which syllable connected his body
to that of a hummingbird's
to have its eyes and speed,
why it was essential to be able
to see and avoid the aura
of hiding women. their huts
were visible along the hills,
draining the snow of its water,
making the winter's visit much
shorter, but deep inside he knew
he had no regrets. the way
the bird sat, the way it cleaned
its wings, the way it breathed
told him he had kept his distance.
the winter had been friendly.
with only one dream to think
about, he collected the cold bodies
to muskrats given to him
by well-wishers and proceeded
to cut open their bellies,
carve their bodies into boats,
and positioned their bellies
to the sky, hoping for snow.
it was easy every time his
food ran out to hobble over
to the road knowing he'd get
a ride into town for groceries
and back making little use
of his cane. it wasn't unusual

for him to look out his window
and see families bringing him
whiskey, bright-colored
blankets, assorted towels,
canned triangles of ham.
his trunks were full
of the people's gratitude.
through the summer and fall,
he named babies, led clan
feasts, and he never refused whenever
families asked him to speak
to the charred mouths of young
bodies that had died drunk.
he was always puzzled to see
their life seeping through
the bandages, the fresh oil
of their long hair,
the distorted and confused
shadows struggling to catch up
to their deaths. he spoke
to suicides just as he would
to anyone who had died peacefully.
he knew it was wrong to ask them
to go on, but he couldn't refuse
lives that were already lost.
everybody counted on him.
each knew that if they died
within his time, he would
be the one to hand them
their last dream,
the grandfather of all
dream.